WOMEN in POLITICS

Queen Noor

Women in Politics

Madeleine Albright

Benazir Bhutto

Hillary Rodham Clinton

Elizabeth Dole

Nancy Pelosi

Queen Noor

WOMEN in POLITICS

Queen Noor

Susan Muaddi Darraj

CHELSEA HOUSE
PUBLISHERS
A Haights Cross Communications Company
Philadelphia

CHELSEA HOUSE PUBLISHERS
VP, NEW PRODUCT DEVELOPMENT Sally Cheney
DIRECTOR OF PRODUCTION Kim Shinners
CREATIVE MANAGER Takeshi Takahashi
MANUFACTURING MANAGER Diann Grasse

Staff for QUEEN NOOR
EXECUTIVE EDITOR Lee Marcott
ASSOCIATE EDITOR Kate Sullivan
PRODUCTION EDITOR Megan Emery
PHOTO EDITOR Sarah Bloom
SERIES & COVER DESIGNER Terry Mallon
LAYOUT 21st Century Publishing and Communications, Inc.

A Haights Cross Communications ✦ Company

www.chelseahouse.com

First Printing

9 8 7 6 5 4 3 2 1

Library of Congress Cataloging-in-Publication Data

Darraj, Susan Muaddi.
  Queen Noor / by Susan Muaddi Darraj.
    v. cm. — (Women in politics)
  Includes index.
  Includes bibliographical references.
  Contents: A privileged childhood — Awakenings — Seeing the world
— Jordan — Rough beginnings — War on many fronts — Everything
changes — Flying solo.
  ISBN 0-7910-7736-5 — ISBN 0-7910-8002-1 (pbk.) 1. Noor, Queen,
consort of Hussein, King of Jordan, 1951—-Juvenile literature. [1. Noor,
Queen, consort of Hussein, King of Jordan, 1951- 2. Kings, queens,
rulers, etc. 3. Women—Biography.] I. Title. II. Series.
  DS154.52.N87D37 2003
  956.9504'4'092—dc22

                                                  2003023915

Table of Contents

An American Dream

1890–1955

Even on their honeymoon, Queen Noor couldn't have King Hussein all to herself. The royal couple, who married in June 1978, spent the first half of their honeymoon in Scotland and the second in England. It was a most unusual time: the carefully planned weeks of romantic bliss quickly turned into work sessions for Hussein, who had to attend to the administration of his kingdom. That's what life is like when one is married to a king. And there was worse to come. At one point, their romantic holiday became a dangerous escapade; as Noor later remembered, "We nearly died on our honeymoon. Literally."[1]

At the Gleneagles resort in the Perthshire region of Scotland, Noor and Hussein shared a bungalow that featured an elaborate mahogany bed, fireplaces, and high ceilings. One

Practically over night, the life of the beautiful Lisa Halaby changed forever when she married King Hussein of Jordan and became Queen Noor. The young bride would soon learn that being queen was not entirely a fairy tale; she would be stepmother to the king's eight children from previous marriages and would work hard for her adopted country.

night, shortly after their arrival, a heater broke down in their suite, filling the bungalow with toxic fumes. Overcome by the bitter odor, the two tried to escape, but the king's security guards had locked the sturdy door from the outside and couldn't hear the couple's desperate pounding. Struggling to remain conscious, Hussein and Noor dialed random numbers until they reached a hotel telephone operator, who alerted the guards. Upon being rescued, Noor remembered, "We gulped in fresh air in painful gasps." [2]

That a king who had survived so many assassination attempts should nearly be killed by a broken hotel heater and miscommunication with his security guards seemed ridiculous. Noor, however, was learning a sobering lesson: being shadowed by security guards around the clock would be the least difficult adjustment she would have to make as a member of the royal court.

Another lesson Noor learned on her honeymoon was that she had married a man whose time was beyond his control. Since becoming king at the age of 18, Hussein had devoted his life to his country. His time and attention were necessarily divided between the people of his nation and the people in his family. He had also been married three times previously— Noor was his fourth wife—and the new queen had inherited a large family of eight stepchildren. With a husband pulled in so many directions, she wondered how he would ever have time for her. At one point, mired in paperwork, the king suggested to a restless Noor that she go shopping with his secretary. "He presumed that I loved to shop, but this was my honeymoon, and I wanted to spend it getting to know my husband." [3] Her frustration increased slowly, but steadily.

After they left the rolling hills and green fields of Scotland, the royal couple visited Castlewood, the king's country home on the outskirts of London, England. It was one of many homes in Europe and the United States that Hussein owned, one in which he especially enjoyed relaxing. Yet, even here, Noor could not spend time alone with Hussein. His three youngest children, Ali, Abir, and Haya, joined them on picnics in the country and on excursions to London. A few days into the second half of this most unorthodox of honeymoons,

Hussein's oldest son, Abdullah, joined them as well. Abdullah, who was a high school freshman at Deerfield Academy in Massachusetts, flew to England from the United States to spend time with his father—a rare treat—and to meet his new stepmother.[4] Noor was happy for them, especially for Hussein. She knew he enjoyed spending time with his children and was disappointed that his tight schedule barely afforded him the opportunity to do so. At Castlewood, Hussein and his eldest son enjoyed playfully roughhousing, arm wrestling, and laughing together. Even though it was still her honeymoon, Noor made herself fade into the background so as not to interfere.

But for the new bride, this honeymoon had offered a dim picture of her future. Much of her time would be spent raising Hussein's large family, visiting with dignitaries and heads of state, and even shopping with the king's secretary. There would be all too little time to spend with her ever-occupied husband himself. One night in Castlewood, things proved too much for the new bride. In a rare moment of emotional weakness, the tearful queen of Jordan called her mother in the United States and cried, "I feel like coming home."

GROWING UP HALABY

Halab (which means "milk" in Arabic) is the name of the ancient Syrian city known in the West as Aleppo. Founded as early as the second millennium B.C., Aleppo is famed in the Middle East as a major hub of culture and the arts.[5] Located in northern Syria, close to the Turkish border, Aleppo is the second oldest continuously inhabited city in the world. It has a distinctly eastern atmosphere, a maze of narrow streets all twined around the famous citadel or ancient fortress, which sits at the city's heart. Gertrude Bell, the famed English traveler, once said of the city, "If there be a better gate to Asia than Aleppo, I do not know it."[6] It is in Aleppo where one can trace Queen Noor's ancestral heritage.

Around 1890, Najeeb Halaby ("Halaby" means "one from

Halab") and his family traveled from their native Syria to Lebanon, the neighboring country that sits on the Mediterranean. It was the first milestone of a much longer journey, an eagerly anticipated transatlantic voyage to the United States. With his mother Almas and his older brother Habib, the young Najeeb sailed from the Lebanese capital city of Beirut to New York to start a new life.

The brothers barely spoke English, but they were determined to succeed in America, the land where the streets were allegedly paved with gold, the land where hardworking and clever immigrants could "strike it rich." On the ship, they carried large carpetbags in which they had packed "oriental rugs, damask fabric, copperware, and jewelry—fine wares from the old country to sell and trade while they adjusted to a new life."[7] Najeeb Halaby (later to become the grandfather of Queen Noor) was only twelve years old.

In Maine, Najeeb met Frances Cleveland—the wife of President Grover Cleveland—and enticed her with his finely crafted wares from Syria. She was impressed with the young man's charm and work ethic, and she wrote him letters of introduction to several well-connected people. It was all that the Halaby brothers needed to begin their future in their adopted country. America was, indeed, the land where dreams came true. They established a profitable and successful import-export business, though the work of managing it eventually fell to Habib. The younger Najeeb eventually set his sights on Texas, attracted by stories of wealth to be made in the oil fields.

Najeeb was successful in Texas, and it appears that Texas like him as much as he liked it. Years later, the granddaughter who had never met him heard him described as handsome and gallant. Though the 1920 census lists Najeeb Halaby as an "oil broker," it does not seem that he made his fortune in oil although he seems to have struck it rich in other ways in Dallas.[8] In 1914, he met and married Laura Wilkins, an interior decorator, and together they founded Halaby Galleries,

ARAB IMMIGRATION TO AMERICA

Arabs have been part of the cultural fabric of the United States for centuries, and members of the Arab-American community have contributed to the extraordinary achievements of the nation. In fact, history shows that Arabs arrived in America as early as the 15th century with the Spanish explorers. In the late 1800s, they were represented at expositions and fairs in big cities like Philadelphia and Chicago, an indication that they must have been a large and prominent community.

The most significant numbers of Arabs arrived in the United States during the Great Migration, which occurred between 1880 and 1924. It was an important period in the history of the nation, marked by the immigration of more than 20 million people from around the world. This immigration included Arabs from Lebanon, Syria, Palestine, and elsewhere in the Middle East, so that more than 200,000 Arabs lived in America by 1924. By 1892, these Arab immigrants established an Arab-language newspaper; by 1923, they had also built the first mosque in the country, located near Detroit, and had erected several Arab churches across the nation.*

Many more Arab-Americans arrived in the second half of the 1900s, and they continued to make a positive impact on the nation. Some of the most well-known Americans of Arab ancestry, in addition to Queen Noor of Jordan, include actors Salma Hayek, Kathy Najimy, Yasmeen Bleeth, Shannon Elizabeth, and Tony Shalhoub; singers Paula Abdul, Tiffany, and Shakira; sports star Doug Flutie; consumer rights activist Ralph Nader; the late comedian Danny Thomas; fashion designer Joseph Abboud; doctor and inventor of the heart pump, Dr. Michael Debakey; and Nobel prizewinners Dr. Ahmed Zewail and Dr. Elias Corey.**

There are currently over 3 million people of Arab descent in the United States.

* "The History of Arab Immigration to the U.S." ADC.org, http://www.adc.org/education/AAImmigration.htm

** "Arab Americans: Making a Difference." Arab American Institute, http://www.aaiusa.org/famous_arab_americans.htm

which "combined his import-export skills with her love of art and decorating."[9] Before long, Halaby Galleries became the place the wealthy and elite of Dallas sought advice about their design ideas and purchases.

Laura Wilkins was a local Texan girl, the daughter of a rancher, and her marriage to a Middle Eastern immigrant—especially one who refused, unlike other immigrants, to Anglicize his "exotic" surname—must have raised some eyebrows in the community. While allowing people to call him "Ned" rather than "Najeeb," the only other major concession the Syrian immigrant made to his new culture was to convert from the Greek Orthodox Christian faith to his wife's Christian Science faith. (While the majority of Arabs are Muslim, Najeeb and the Halabys belonged to the small percentage of Arabs who are Christian). Despite Najeeb's retention of his Arab identity and the community's general suspicion of Arabs and most other foreigners, he was largely accepted in Dallas and was eventually invited to join the exclusive Dallas Athletic Club.[10]

Najeeb and Laura had only one child, a boy they named Najeeb after his proud father. Born on September 19, 1915, little Najeeb would become the center of their world. As Halaby Galleries was successful and becoming increasingly profitable, the child enjoyed a privileged life. He attended private school and basked in the undivided attention of his mother and the adoration of his father.

Tragedy struck when the young boy was only thirteen years old, almost the same age the elder Najeeb was when he crossed the Atlantic to move to the United States. Because the Christian Science faith insisted on spiritual healing and rejected medical care, the elder Najeeb did not immediately consult a doctor when he developed an apparent case of strep throat during the winter of 1928. As Noor recounts in her autobiography, "Najeeb senior was quite weak when he finally went into the hospital, where he developed an infection and died" shortly before Christmas that same year.[11] Now a single mother and a grieving widow, Laura sold Halaby Galleries and moved to California to seek a better, more stable future. She eventually married again. Her new husband was Urban Koen, "an affluent Frenchman from New Orleans."[12] but the marriage lasted only a few years. Laura was utterly devoted to her young son, and hostility between Najeeb and his stepfather eventually resulted in the failure of the marriage.

With the money left from the sale of the Halaby Galleries, Laura made sure that "Jeeb's" life was active and full. He attended the finest schools, and after graduating from high school, he enrolled at Stanford University and later attended Yale Law School. Though he earned his law degree from a prestigious Ivy League university, his career interests lay in elsewhere.

When Najeeb was a boy, his father had taken his only son to downtown Dallas to a ticker-tape parade held for Charles Lindbergh, the first person to conquer transatlantic flight. It was 1927, and public excitement about the potential for air transportation was high, affecting young Najeeb deeply. Seeing Lindbergh was a highlight of his childhood: "I remember jumping up and down and screaming in the backseat of the family [car] as Lindbergh rode past . . . his dignified, youthful appearance—almost saintly looking—was uplifting."[13] Intrigued by flying, Najeeb Halaby pursued a career in aviation after law school. During World War II, he test piloted several airplanes, especially bombers, for the aviation division of the Lockheed Corporation. He also served in the Carrier Fighter Test Branch of the Navy, testing over fifty types of planes and aircraft for the military. As Noor later noted, "My father had the temperament so necessary to a test pilot. He was bold, confident in his technical skills, focused, and a risk taker, as well as possessing an aviator's broad perspective and inherent optimism."[14] Najeeb Halaby was, indeed, an optimist—a man who worked hard and possessed the same fervent enthusiasm for life exemplified by his late father. While living in Washington, D.C., shortly after World War II had ended, he met a woman who shared his outlook—Doris

Carlquist. A striking tall blonde woman of Swedish ancestry, Doris, like Najeeb, was intrigued by politics and believed in making the world a better place. "Like me," Najeeb recalled, "she had stars in her eyes about peace and international understanding."[15] Doris, the daughter of a broker whose business had been destroyed by the 1929 stock market crash, was independent. Her mother had died when Doris was only fifteen years old, and thus, Doris and Najeeb shared the sad experience of losing a parent at a young age. Though devastated by her mother's death, Doris enrolled in college but dropped out because of lack of funds. Her father could not support her, and Doris lived with assorted relatives while working at various jobs.

Doris and Najeeb fell in love, marrying on December 24, 1946. Doris gave up her job, as custom dictated at the time for upper-middle-class women, and Najeeb pursued in earnest his ideals of a more understanding world. He was especially interested in the Middle East. In a way, he was returning to his ethnic roots by focusing on the region of the world from which his father had emigrated half a century earlier. It was the Middle East that, more than any other part of the globe, was undergoing a major change.

After World War II, the region was transformed (whether for better or worse is still debated by scholars). Most of the Middle East had been occupied and colonized by the British, whose empire in the Arab world stretched as far back as the early 1800s. Colonialism had proved disastrous for Arabs and Muslims; living under foreign domination had caused Arab society, economy, and education to generally stagnate. However, the end of World War II presaged the end of European rule in the Middle East, and Arab nations from North Africa to Jordan to Saudi Arabia welcomed independence. "When the United Nations was formed in 1945," writes Middle East historian Albert Hourani, "the independent Arab states became members of it."[16] Essentially, the Middle Eastern states were young and unestablished, requiring stable economies and trade relationships with other nations in order to survive. After his marriage to Doris Carlquist, Najeeb Halaby spent an entire summer in Saudi Arabia, advising King Saud bin Abdul Aziz on civil aviation matters. Oil had been discovered in Saudi Arabia only a few years earlier, and Najeeb saw the potential for development of the country. Upon his return to Washington, D.C., Najeeb encouraged the State Department (for whom he had conducted previous work in research and intelligence after the end of the war) to boost its support—military, financial, and technical—of the gulf nation. Steadily gaining influence and making advantageous connections in powerful circles, Najeeb was making himself indispensable in political circles in Washington. He left the State Department around 1947 to join the newly formed Department of Defense, and to work for James Forrestal, who had been appointed first secretary of defense. Later, Najeeb was recruited by the administration of President Harry Truman to help organize the North Atlantic Treaty Organization (NATO). He also became the deputy assistant secretary of defense for international security affairs under the administration of President Dwight Eisenhower.[17] Political and governmental administrative work, however, paid little and was exhausting. Though a workaholic by nature, even Najeeb realized he was severely overworked. In addition, he now had a young family whose future he needed to secure.

A PERIPATETIC CHILDHOOD: 1951–1956

Lisa Najeeb Halaby, the future Queen Noor, was born on August 23, 1951, in Washington, D.C. The first child born to Najeeb and Doris, Lisa would have two other siblings close to her age: a brother, Christian, born in 1953, and a sister, Alexa, born in 1955. All three Halaby children had American names, though Doris had wanted to name the eldest girl Camille, after one of Najeeb's dearest uncles who lived in South America and who was a good friend to the young couple. However, Camille himself insisted that his nephew's children be given names that were not Arabic or foreign sounding in any way, so as to help them assimilate more easily to American culture. This seems unusual, given that Najeeb, like his father before him, never changed his name.

In 1953, Najeeb and Doris moved their young family from Washington, D.C., to New York, where Najeeb accepted a job offer from Laurance Rockefeller, who owned a significant share of Eastern Airlines. Najeeb would learn "a great deal about the aviation business working for the Rockefeller brothers, immersing himself in the corporate financing of airlines and the municipal funding of airports, setting up a task force to reorganize and modernize the country's rapidly growing airways and airport systems," wrote his daughter Lisa years later.[18] Eventually, due to corporate squabbles, Najeeb moved on to accept a position as an executive vice president of Servo-Mechanisms, Inc., a manufacturer of "electronic subsystems."[19] It meant another move for the growing Halaby family—this time, to California.

Lisa's childhood was already an unusual one, but shuffling around the nation from home to home in response to her father's employment changes made things even more difficult. "We moved often during my childhood," she recalls, "and the constant changes reinforced my natural reserve."[20] In New York, for example, she attended a nursery school close to the Halabys' East 73rd Street apartment, but being in a classroom filled with other children only increased her shyness. She was so introverted and reluctant to engage in play and conversation that a concerned Doris Halaby consulted a child psychologist about what she considered her eldest daughter's "alarming" behavior. The psychologist apparently told Doris not to worry, but Lisa would remain painfully shy into adulthood. Whenever the family moved, she found the process of adjusting to a new life very unsettling. "Time and again, I would find myself on the outside looking in—watching, studying, learning—having to familiarize myself with unfamiliar people and communities."[21] Moving to California did not alter Lisa's quiet, reserved nature (her father,

As a child, Lisa Halaby moved often as her father pursued a career in aviation technology and management. Lisa, pictured here with her mother and father, would later recall living in California as among the happiest times in her life.

who was naturally outgoing and assertive, thought she was "aloof"), but it did mark a happy change in her childhood. Lisa was five years old when Najeeb's job at Servo-Mechanisms prompted the move to Los Angeles, and the Halabys rented a house in the posh Brentwood district. The house had a large swimming pool, where Lisa learned to swim, and a lush garden, where she enjoyed walking and breathing in the crisp scent of the citrus trees. They remained in the area but moved several times before finally settling in Santa Monica, moving into an old Victorian house with a magnificent view of the sparkling Pacific Ocean.

It was in this house, with a view of the ocean and the feel of the California sun, that Lisa would spend some of her happiest—and most challenging—years.

2

California Girl
1956–1970

In her parents' home in California, young Lisa had everything a girl could want: fresh air, warm sun, the sound of the ocean surf to lull her to sleep at night. The house itself was filled with delights to stimulate her imagination. "With an expansive, tumbledown garden bordered at the end by a row of dilapidated pigeon cages, it was a wonderful house to grow up in: eccentric and full of character," she wrote, describing its "high ceilings, an atrium filled with plants, a billiard room, a porch with a huge swing, and a spacious, romantic attic in which my father . . . assembled a puppet theater swathed in tiny lights."[22] Ever the quiet child, Lisa spent hours playing alone in the empty lot beside the house.

The house also featured a large library, where Najeeb kept all his books—a wide-ranging, eclectic collection that included everything from Khalil Gibran to Nevil Shute. Lisa (who found the *Encyclopædia Brittanica* especially absorbing) enjoyed roaming through the stacks of books, then taking one outside to read underneath a large magnolia tree on the Halaby property. It was in this library, poring over all the books and magazines, that Lisa's love of adventure and learning was first sparked. "I would flip through copies of *National Geographic* and gaze longingly at the globe that helped me chart my parents' international trips." [23]

Indeed, her parents were quite busy, due to the important corporate and business responsibilities of Najeeb's job as executive vice president of the manufacturing company. Najeeb had inherited his father's entrepreneurial spirit and his work ethic, so much so that his determination to succeed and provide for his young family occasionally prevented him from connecting with his daughter. "He sought perfection and never seemed satisfied," she recalls, and attributes some of her childhood feelings of inadequacy to this tension. Her position as the eldest of the three Halaby children did not ease the burden to achieve that often befalls the eldest, and Najeeb's high expectations sometimes wounded her deeply. Once, after having taken Lisa to see an eye doctor, Doris explained to her husband that Lisa had a vision problem and would probably need glasses. Najeeb denied it, and "tested" Lisa by holding his copy of *Time* magazine up to her face, asking her to read it. Though he eventually held the magazine very close to her face, Lisa could not even make out the large font of the headlines. Despite this, Najeeb refused to accept that Lisa needed glasses, because in his mind, as Lisa surmised, he wondered, "How could one of his children be so flawed?" [24]

In truth, Najeeb—rarely satisfied and full of ambition—was working harder than ever, and it was paying off like never before. He left Servo-Mechanisms to practice law (and make use of his Yale law degree) and to start his own technology company. However, things changed in 1960, when the youthful and popular John F. Kennedy was elected president. Not long after the election, Najeeb was approached by the president-elect's brother-in-law, Sargent Shriver (a Yale classmate of Najeeb), and another of Kennedy's close associates. He was invited to accept an important position in the new administration—as director of the Federal Aviation Administration. Najeeb's years of government service, including testing planes for the military, and his widely-recognized genius for aviation, as well as his management experience and knowledge of the law, made him a perfect candidate for the post.

Najeeb, however, hesitated to accept it. "He was finally making good money," his daughter explained, "and was not in a rush to return to the relative penury of public service." [25] In addition, the position of FAA Director would necessitate relocating his young family once again to Washington, D.C. After considering all of this, Najeeb respectfully declined the offer.

It is a testament to Najeeb's intelligence, stellar reputation, and solid work ethic that the new administration did not accept his initial refusal as a final answer. In a private meeting on January 19, 1961, just one day before his inauguration as president, John F. Kennedy himself persuaded Najeeb to accept the post. The next day, as Kennedy took the oath of office and was sworn in as the 35th president of the United States, Najeeb and Doris Halaby watched the proceedings up close from their seats behind the podium. Najeeb Halaby, the son of an immigrant, had continued his father's American dream, and the Halaby star was rising higher than ever.

The Halaby children, back in California, saw their parents on television and were thrilled. At the same time, they probably wondered if this meant yet another move.

TURMOIL IN THE WORLD: 1961–1963

Not surprisingly, moving back to Washington, D.C., proved difficult for Lisa, who was ten years old. She missed California, did not adjust right away to the more challenging school

In 1961, President Kennedy persuaded a reluctant Najeeb Halaby to take a government post as head of the Federal Aviation Administration. The job change resulted in a substantial pay cut from Halaby's career as a lawyer and the head of his own technology company. It also meant yet another move for the Halaby family, this time to Washington, D.C.

curriculum, and had trouble making friends. She described herself during these years in very unflattering terms: "I was . . . tall for my age, scrawny and awkward, and dependent on Coke-bottle-thick glasses."[26] However, these next few years in the nation's capital would be Lisa's formative years, when she developed her own sense of self and her identity. It was also the time when she learned more about the world and her role in it.

Her grandmother, Laura, had moved east with the family. Najeeb was, after all, her only child, and she wanted to stay close to him and his wife and children. She lived nearby, on a farm in Virginia, south of Washington, D.C. Laura Halaby's farm provided Lisa with a break from the rigors of home life, where she had to be on her best behavior while her parents entertained prominent guests and visitors. On her grandmother's farm, Lisa enjoyed horseback riding and exploring the countryside. It was during one of these pleasant excursions that she had her first encounter with stark poverty.

Lisa later recalled an experience she had riding near a small farming community of migrants: "I felt absolute shock, fear, and then utter helplessness and guilt as I was confronted by the black, hopeless stares of migrant children and their families seeking shade from the pitiless noonday sun."[27] It was a moment she would never forget, and it made her aware of and sympathetic to the plight of the poor.

Though the Halabys were hardly that destitute, Lisa soon became aware of her family's financial troubles for the first time. Returning to government service was personally rewarding for Najeeb, but his fears about the move quickly proved to be well founded: the salary he earned working in the private sector was reduced by two-thirds.[28] The family had to be careful how they spent their money, but Najeeb refused to compromise on certain expenses. For example, he and Doris insisted that their daughters and son attend private school; thus, Lisa enrolled at the National Cathedral School for girls, where her classmates included the daughters of other members of the Kennedy administration. However, the burden of education and other necessary expenses worried Lisa's father. In a rare moment of closeness, he once confessed to her that "he was struggling under a terrible burden of debt and yet was happier and more fulfilled in public service than in any more lucrative career."[29]

He also struggled with other burdens. His marriage to Doris, under much strain, was barely surviving. The two did not have as much in common as they had once thought. Their family situations and ethnic backgrounds were very different. Furthermore, Najeeb worked long hours, and he and Doris had trouble seeing eye-to-eye on many issues, which led to quarrels. "The constant tension between them permeated the household," their oldest daughter recalled.[30]

There was also the ever-intense prejudice in America against foreigners and a wariness of those from the Middle East. Despite his success, the fact remained that Najeeb was an Arab-American, with an olive complexion, Middle Eastern features, and dark hair—a man who held a prestigious position in a field and a political realm dominated by white men. Perhaps the moment that clarified for Lisa how differently her father was regarded was when she read the following question in a local newspaper's quiz: "What is a Najeeb Elias Halaby: animal, vegetable, or mineral?"[31] It was a reminder that the Halabys would never quite fit in.

The time of the Kennedy administration (1961–1963) was one of great excitement and enthusiasm for America's youth. However, these years also spelled some of the worst social upheaval in the United States. But as the nation grappled with the fear of nuclear war, the threat of communism, and the scars of racism, Kennedy helped channel the frustrations of young Americans into positive action.

One of Kennedy's most popular and most enduring programs was the Peace Corps, a program that invited young Americans to spend time working in various regions around the globe fighting hunger, illiteracy, poverty and other afflictions while learning about the world and spreading a positive message about America's values. Spurred by Kennedy's vision for a better nation and a more peaceful world, America's youth became infected with the ambition to make Kennedy's vision a reality.

Lisa herself became caught up in the contagious idealism, and dreamed of enlisting in the Peace Corps when she was old enough. During this time, she also became a firm supporter of civil rights. One night, while spending time with her grandmother, Lisa watched the race riots at the University of Mississippi unfold on television. It was the fall of 1962, and the question of segregation had found an opponent in Kennedy, who wanted to integrate American schools and public institutions in a peaceful, nonconfrontational way. Unfortunately, with frustrations and anger at a peak over the issue, the two goals seemed mutually exclusive.

In 1962, James Meredith, a Black American and a nine-year veteran of the U.S. Air Force, attempted to enroll at the exclusively white University of Mississippi, known as "Ole Miss."[32] The university had rejected Meredith's application, despite his proven solid academic record. When he took his case to the federal courts, the law voted on his side; on September 10, 1962, the Supreme Court of the United States ordered the university to allow Meredith to enroll.[33] A furious mob tried to prevent Meredith from enrolling, endangering his life and the lives of his police escorts as well. Trapped in a dormitory, Meredith and the police officers were threatened with Molotov cocktails, guns, and bottles. Ross Barnett, the governor of Mississippi, was staunchly opposed to integration and did little to stop the chaos. In fact, the governor publicly proclaimed he would never allow Meredith to be admitted to the university.

As Lisa Halaby and her grandmother Laura Halaby watched the news of the riot developing on television, the young Lisa, who was only eleven years old, sympathized with Meredith. Like other Americans, she waited to see whether President Kennedy would order in the National Guard to quell the mob, enforce the law, and allow Meredith to enroll. (The president would eventually order in 33,000 federal troops to control the situation). At one point, the Reverend Martin Luther King, Jr. appeared on television, strongly supporting Meredith and applauding his bravery. "Isn't he wonderful?" Lisa gushed to her grandmother. Laura Halaby agreed, but as Lisa recalled, "it quickly became apparent that she was praising George Wallace, the racist governor of Alabama, who had spoken a few minutes earlier, and the realization triggered an excruciating argument." [34] Lisa spent the rest of the night in her room, and believed that her relationship with her dear grandmother would never regain its once-special quality. However, she was learning to form her own opinions and defend her ideals and values. In 1961, Lisa joined the Student Nonviolent Coordinating Committee (SNCC), established a year earlier in order to protest segregation in public spaces. Students of all races and ethnic backgrounds staged "sit-ins" in parks, theaters, public restrooms and other places where white and black Americans were segregated. "We sang 'We Shall Overcome,'" wrote Lisa, "and we meant it." [35]

Lisa was only twelve years old when Martin Luther King made his famous "I Have a Dream" speech on August 28, 1963, but the passion for social justice had already been stirred in her soul. Despite the fact that many of the adults in her life—the people who were part of her privileged world—seemed more annoyed than inspired by the Civil Rights movement, it was a time that would permanently affect Lisa and shape her future, idealistic vision of the importance of social equity and justice.

CHANGES: 1963–1970

On November 22, 1963, the pillar that had propped up that idealistic vision collapsed. "While crossing Woodley Road with my classmates in our way to the athletic field," she wrote in her memoir, "I heard a devastating report from Dallas, Texas, on the crossing guard's radio. President Kennedy's motorcade had come under fire. . . . When the National Cathedral's bells began to toll their tragic message later in the day, we were devastated.

It was inconceivable that our dashing young president could have been in harm's way." [36]

The assassination of President Kennedy, who had been shot twice while seated beside his wife in his motorcade, stunned the nation. Especially stunned were the young people who idolized him. Secret Service agents entered the classrooms of the National Cathedral School and the daughters of newly sworn-in President Johnson were taken away for their own protection. Lisa and the other children of members of Kennedy's administration reported to the headmistress's office, where they were offered updates and reassurance. However,

CIVIL RIGHTS MOVEMENT

Starting in the 1950s, Black Americans in the United States began an organized, concentrated effort to gain their equal rights. Though Abraham Lincoln had officially emancipated the slaves during the Civil War in the mid-1800s, Black Americans did not enjoy basic everyday rights accorded white citizens. In fact, they had become the victims of segregation. Segregation meant that they were forced to attend separate schools, sit in separate sections of public transportation vehicles, and even drink from different public water fountains than white Americans. In May 1954, the Supreme Court ruled that segregation in public schools was illegal and unconstitutional. More than a year later, a black woman, Rosa Parks, refused to give up her seat on a bus to a white passenger, an act of defiance that resulted in her arrest, a year-long boycott of the bus system in Montgomery, Alabama, and demonstrations against racist practices. The Civil Rights movement was born.

The movement took different shapes and forms, and was most notable for its nonviolent nature. Led by the Reverend Dr. Martin Luther King, the Southern Christian Leadership Conference (SCLC) organized many of the most widely effective grassroots actions against racism. Their tactics included children's marches, sit-ins, peaceful protests, no amount of reassurance could restore Lisa's optimism. "President Kennedy's death shattered my world," she wrote.[37]

The assassination also affected her family tremendously. Though Najeeb Halaby continued to serve as the FAA director under President Lyndon Johnson, he was falling more and more deeply into debt because of the meager pay earned from public service. In 1965, Halaby resigned and accepted an offer to head Pan Am Airways, which meant moving the Halabys yet again, this time back to New York.

In New York, despite her ardent protests, Lisa attended the Chapin School, an elite academy for girls. Najeeb and Doris

and prayers—all meant to force America to realize the evils of racism and to bring about equality for all citizens. Another very influential organization, the Student Nonviolent Coordinating Committee (SNCC), used similar tactics and enjoyed equal success. SNCC, as it was known, reached out to both black students as well as white students, in an effort to eliminate racism. Queen Noor became active in SNCC as a young woman; she joined the organization in 1961.*

Most civil rights activists faced severe challenges and were often the targets of violence and hatred. The entire country experienced a tumultuous several years, the climax of which was the 1963 march on Washington, during which 250,000 people demanded equality for all and Dr. King delivered his famous, powerful "I Have a Dream" speech. A year later, President Lyndon Johnson signed the Civil Rights Act of 1964 into law, banning segregation and putting into effect a foundation upon which other anti-racist measures would be built.**

* Her Majesty Queen Noor Al-Hussein, *Leap of Faith: Memoirs of an Unexpected Life.* New York: Miramax Books, 2003.

** "Civil Rights Timeline." Infoplease.com. *http://www.infoplease.com/spot/ civilrightstimeline1.html* wanted to remove Lisa from an environment where the social rage over civil rights, the Vietnam War, and other social issues that were exploding across the country would affect her. Perhaps the fact that Lisa was "increasingly vocal about my opposition to America's military involvement in Vietnam" spurred her parents to choose a sheltered environment.[38] Chapin was not only protective, but almost sealed off from the rest of society. "The world was held at arm's length at Chapin, with no student involvement in the debate over Vietnam or the civil rights movement or, indeed, anything that smacked of dissent."[39] She remembers that "Chapin felt like a strait jacket," and she often rebelled against the rules.[40] Despite Lisa's misery, her parents felt it was the best choice for her. Perhaps they were also attracted to Chapin because of its former famous students, such as Jacqueline Bouvier, the widow of President Kennedy.

Nevertheless, her parents eventually relented, and for her last two years of high school, a grateful Lisa was permitted to transfer to the Concord Academy, where discipline was the order of the day. The practical atmosphere of the academy attracted Lisa; Concord's rules were strict, even old-fashioned, meting out punishments like chopping wood for missing class.[41] Lisa thrived in the new environment, and later wrote, "Academic life [at Concord] was extremely stimulating, and expectations were high, but more important to me, the school placed a high premium on individualism and personal responsibility."[42] The atmosphere suited the quiet, thoughtful, and deeply conscientious young woman perfectly.

After high school, Lisa planned to attend Stanford University, which had accepted her for the class of 1973. For Lisa, Stanford was not only an exceptional academic institution; it was also a means for her to return to California, the setting of some of her happiest childhood memories. However, she also received an acceptance letter from Princeton, which had been, throughout its long and distinguished history, a strictly all-male institution. The 1973 class would be the first co-ed class in the university's history, as it had finally decided to open its classroom doors to female students. Lisa accepted the challenge Princeton offered, rationalizing that she would try it out for two years and then transfer to Stanford if she was unhappy.

Princeton proved to be a challenge indeed. Not only were female students outnumbered (by a ratio of 1 to 22) by males, but Lisa found herself an outsider and had trouble fitting in. "The reserve I had acquired in nursery school to cope with my social awkwardness led to all sorts of misconceptions," she remembered.[43] Classmates accused her of being snobbish and self-important, and "it did not help that, in a flurry of publicity, my father was finally named the new CEO and president of Pan Am soon after the fall term began, further cementing my 'unapproachable' image."[44]

During this time, Lisa also became more aware of her Arab heritage, though in a negative way. In her memoir, she recalls the day some upperclassmen on campus harassed her about her ethnic background.[45] Later, when she had graduated from Princeton, Lisa would go in search of that heritage, to find its meaning in the hope of finding herself.

3

Student of the World
1971–1978

Lisa excelled at Princeton, despite the occasional evidence of intolerance by classmates about her ethnic identity. However, other tensions accompanied her first two years there, including the uneasiness of being one of only a few women on campus: "We were definitely in an awkward situation," she writes, because of male students, "whose previous experience with women on campus was as weekend attractions."[46] Other concerns, however, reverberated on a global scale.

The Vietnam War raged on the other side of the world, and the numbers of Americans soldiers returning home in body bags—as well as the atrocities occurring against the Vietnamese people—shook America's college campuses. Princeton was no exception, for which Lisa, whose chief complaint against the Chapin School was its isolationist tone, was grateful. Absorbed in social causes and passionate about human rights, Lisa jumped into the action, taking part in fasts and other nonviolent forms of protest. Other universities across the nation were experiencing similar upheaval. At Kent State University, for example, the Ohio National Guard fired on crowds of student protesters, killing four people. "The outrage was immediate," remembers Lisa. "The entire Princeton campus went on strike, and exams were cancelled. During a protest at the Institute of Defense Analyses, we were teargassed by anti-riot police."[47] She admits that the military and foreign policy of the United States at the time left her conflicted. "While I loved my country, I found my trust in its institutions badly shaken."[48]

Lisa decided that she needed time away from her studies and even from her family in order to sort out her feelings and prioritize her goals. It was 1971, and her inner turmoil reflected that of the outside world. She requested a year's leave of absence and flew to Colorado, planning to work for a year in a bustling ski resort in Aspen and collect her thoughts about the direction in which her future was headed. Her first day of "freedom," however, had anything but a hopeful, optimistic tone. "I arrived during a major winter storm and woke up on the floor of a trailer where I had been offered refuge during the blizzard."[49]

Najeeb Halaby, now the busy CEO and president of Pan Am Airlines, followed her to Aspen, enraged that his eldest daughter would even think to "run away" in such a manner. He found her at a hotel, where she had landed a job cleaning rooms. Nothing he said persuaded her to leave and return to Princeton. "I needed time and space to set my own priorities and to discover if I could survive on my own."[50] Najeeb returned to New York, and Lisa remained in Aspen, taking jobs as a maid, a waitress, and even a gofer, living in a house she rented with some other young women. She also found work with the Aspen Institute, a nonprofit organization that promotes dialogue about international issues through seminars and other educational venues; Lisa worked on the institute's architectural projects and took advantage of lectures and conferences. Always clever, Lisa networked with various people, a habit that would later prove useful. But her time at the Aspen Institute also proved helpful in the short run as well. When she returned to Princeton, she declared her major in architecture and urban planning. "I loved it. It was a captivating, multidisciplinary approach to understanding and addressing the most basic needs of individuals and communities."[51] She had decided on a course of study that suited her passion for serving the needs of society well.

WORKING GIRL: 1974–1976

Lisa graduated from Princeton in 1974, a year later than anticipated due to her time in Aspen. Her first job, with the British firm Llewelyn-Davis, took her to Australia, which thrilled Lisa. Still loyal to her childhood dream of joining the Peace Corps because it would allow her to travel, Lisa wanted to see the world. Her time in Australia lasted one year; then she attended a symposium in Iran, organized by the Aspen Institute. The ruins and scenery of Persepolis, the city hosting the symposium, fascinated Lisa, who had become an avid photographer. When she got the chance to extend her time in Iran, she snatched it. The Shah of Iran had contracted Llewelyn-Davis "to build a model city center on 1,600 acres in north Tehran. . . . The project was an urban planner's fantasy."[52] Lisa moved to Tehran in 1975 to work on the project with approximately 20 other colleagues; at 24, she was the youngest member and the only woman on the team.

As a foreign woman in Iran, Lisa was especially conscious of the role of women in Iranian society, and she concluded that this role was nuanced. While many women wore the chador, full body covering that draped to the ground, underneath the material, many also wore fashionable pants and shoes. It did

Lisa Halaby, never one to refuse a challenge, ultimately accepted a place in Princeton University's first co-educational class in 1969, although she had initially had her heart set on Stanford and a return to California. After her graduation in 1974, she worked as an urban planner in both Australia and Iran before taking a position with her father's newly formed Arab Air Services.

not seem that traditional customs prevented Iranian women from keeping up with the latest trends in fashion. She describes how she never felt threatened or uncomfortable among the Iranian locals, but as a foreigner with bright blonde hair, she was on the receiving end of many odd looks from people she encountered.

Being in Iran also gave her a chance to experience a Middle Eastern (though not an Arab) culture in depth. "My journal from those days describes my feeling that the country seemed to have a split personality. On the one hand, it was very western and cosmopolitan, with a large, well-educated middle class, and on the other, it retained an exotic, Middle Eastern flavor and a dynamic folk culture."[53] More than anything, her time in Tehran made her "aware of a fundamental lack of understanding in the West, especially in the United States, of Middle Eastern culture and the Muslim faith."[54] It was a gap that she would spend the rest of her life trying to bridge.

LIFE IN JORDAN: 1976–1977

In 1972, Najeeb Halaby left Pan Am Airlines. Recognizing his expertise in the field of aviation, several companies and organizations sought him out, including the directors of the recently formed Alia Airlines, the national airline of the Hashemite kingdom of Jordan. In the spring of 1973, Najeeb and Doris accepted an invitation to visit the small desert nation and meet with its charming King Hussein bin Talal, who had been crowned at the young age of eighteen. Hussein spent time with the Halabys, escorting them around in his helicopter. The king, a first-rate pilot himself, established an excellent rapport with Najeeb and recruited the Syrian-American as a consultant for his planned expansion of Alia Airlines, which had been named in honor of his wife, the popular Queen Alia.

In 1976, while traveling to Iran from the United States, Lisa had a chance to see Jordan herself. She fell in love with its culture, atmosphere, music, and energy:

> On that first trip, I explored Amman on foot. Shepherds crossed the downtown streets with their flocks, herding them from one grassy area to another. They were such an ordinary part of life in Amman that no one honked or lost their patience waiting for the streets to clear; animals and their minders had the right of way. I wandered through the marketplace admiring the beautiful inlaid mother-of-pearl objects—frames, chests, and backgammon boards—as well as the cobalt blue, green, and amber vases known as Hebron glass.[55]

The days spent in Jordan were magical and intrigued the young Arab-American, making her curious about her own Arab heritage. She would soon return. Najeeb had opened his own aviation company, Arab Air Services, with offices in Amman, Jordan's bustling capital. He was not only working on Alia Airlines, but was also providing advice and technical support to aviation projects in many other Middle Eastern nations. In the winter of 1976, Jordan acquired its first Boeing 747. A ceremony was planned at the new airport in Amman, and Najeeb invited the 25-year-old Lisa to accompany him to Jordan. Her work in Tehran completed, Lisa was deciding what to do next with her life and was contemplating a career in journalism. She gladly accepted her father's invitation because it meant that she would see Jordan again. She would also have the opportunity to meet its famous royal couple.

Standing on the airport's tarmac, Lisa watched Hussein, his wife Queen Alia, and his daughter, also named Alia, as they chatted with her father. Lisa took a photograph of the king and Najeeb—a photo she would treasure in the years to come. "I never imagined that I would be returning to Jordan just three months later," she writes, "nor did I have any inkling of how fateful that return would be."[56]

Later that year, not finding a journalism job that suited her, Lisa agreed to work for someone she greatly admired: her father. Najeeb's Arab Air Services manager was recovering from an illness, and Lisa accepted the position of replacing him until he could return, a decision which meant relocating temporarily to Amman. Najeeb needed someone he could trust, and given his strict expectations of all his children, Lisa must have been flattered to be asked.

She performed well and explored Jordan further. She

ARCHITECTURE OF JORDAN

Because of her educational background in architecture and urban planning, Queen Noor was especially interested in preserving the architectural treasures of Jordan's ancient cities.

Petra, which lies south of the Dead Sea, dates back to Biblical time, at least to 1200 B.C. However, the city, whose ruins remain today, was probably established around the first century B.C., and under the rule of the Romans, flourished due to its spice trade. The ruins of this ancient city are currently one of the most popular tourist attractions in Jordan. The name "Petra" means "rock," and indeed, the city's buildings and streets are carved out of the red rock of the surrounding mountains.*

Amman, Jordan's capital, is another example of an ancient city, although this is one that continues to thrive. Built across seven hilltops, Amman was originally inhabited over 120,000 years ago, although it changed hands under different ruling armies and leaders until 630, when the Islamic Umayyad dynasty controlled it. Under the Umayyads, Amman thrived for a short while, but then experienced a decline in economy and power, revived only in 1878, when its new rulers, the Turkish Ottomans, relocated a group of Circassians to the region. This small group began rebuilding the city, which steadily grew loved what she saw more than ever. When the manager returned to work, Lisa reluctantly prepared to leave Amman to move back to New York. She had been applying to journalism programs at various schools and was thinking seriously about the change in career track because a journalism career would allow her opportunities to learn and travel the world. As she prepared to fly back to the United States, however, another unique chance presented itself: the opportunity to remain in Jordan to lead one of the divisions of Royal Jordanian Airlines. She would be responsible for overseeing the coordination of the planning and design of the company's facilities.[57] It was

---

in prominence until 1947, when the Hashemite kingdom of Jordan was established with Amman as its capital. True to its mixed origins, Amman features many ancient buildings, reflecting the building styles and architecture of its various rulers, alongside modern ones. The combination can be both haphazard and charming.**

One of Noor's first accomplishments as queen was to develop, along with the Ministry of Public Works, a professional building code for the country. While most nations have a code with which all buildings must comply—in order to protect the land, create standards for safety, and control growth—Jordan lacked such a code until Queen Noor helped develop it. She also worked hard on the research and rehabilitation of many of Jordan's historic edifices, which had been neglected for years. In 1980, she established the National Committee for Public Buildings and Architectural Heritage, an institution dedicated to preserving Jordan's architectural heritage.***

* "A Brief History of Petra." The Petra Great Temple. http://www.brown.edu/Departments/Anthropology/Petra/excavations/history.html.

** "History of Amman." http://www.geocities.com/wesam77/history/amman.html.

*** "Jordan's Architectural Heritage." Official Website of Her Majesty Queen Noor, http://www.noor.gov.jo/main/cjah.htm

an honor to be offered such a prestigious job, especially for one so young.

"As fate would have it," she wrote, "the very next day I received my acceptance letter from Columbia's journalism school," one of the finest and most prestigious programs in the United States.[58] The job with Royal Jordanian Airlines meant she could continue to make use of her architecture and urban planning degree, but New York and a new career start beckoned to her as well.

A BRIEF COURTSHIP: 1978

During her time in Jordan in 1977, Lisa had spent time becoming familiar with the people, the customs, and the politics. She had also seen King Hussein on a few occasions, sometimes during her father's visits and sometimes by chance. The king undoubtedly took notice of the beautiful Arab-American with the long blonde hair.

Life had changed dramatically for the king since the winter of 1976 when he had met Lisa on the tarmac of the airport during the official ceremony marking the acquisition of a Boeing 747. He had, in fact, suffered a tragedy. Queen Alia had been killed in a helicopter crash in February 1977, after deciding to pay a surprise visit to a medical care clinic in a poor region of Jordan. On the way back from the clinic, bad weather and poor visibility caused the helicopter to crash into a hillside. The stricken Hussein built a mosque in her honor and named the Jordanian airport for her. He became deeply depressed, and the entire country, it seemed, mourned the loss of their beloved queen, who had made her mark on the people by being active in charitable and social causes.

In the spring of 1978, Najeeb Halaby arranged for a colleague of his to meet with King Hussein. They both encouraged Lisa to accompany them, but the shy and reserved young woman declined. She went to the Diwan, the king's court, to wait with them before their audience with the king, planning to leave as soon as they were summoned to the king's presence. However, as she later recalled, when the king's chief of protocol arrived to escort Najeeb and his colleague to the king's office, he noticed she was leaving and said, "'The king requests your presence' . . . putting emphasis on the word 'king.'"[59] She could not refuse, and she joined the meeting; afterwards, the king asked her to have lunch at his home, Hashmiya, the next afternoon.[60] A startled Lisa accepted.

Needless to say, Lisa was daunted. While in Amman, she had spent her time living in the posh Inter-Continental Hotel and, as one biography puts it, raising "a few Arab eyebrows by her custom of wearing cutoff blue jeans and being openly affectionate with her businessman boyfriend—all behaviors unbecoming a woman in the Arab culture."[61] She dressed casually, focusing on her work and spending any free time sightseeing and exploring. In trying to immerse herself in the culture and life of Jordan, she suddenly found herself dating its king.

Lisa arrived at Hashmiya for her lunch date with the king at 12:30 in the afternoon, expecting to be overwhelmed by her first visit to his palace. However, her architect's instinct quickly took over, and she quickly concluded that the palace was practically falling apart. The king asked her advice and wondered if she would supervise the needed renovations. When she declined, saying she did not have the necessary qualifications for such work, he seemed baffled. "As I would later learn," she recalled, "people in positions like the king's are usually the last to be given an accurate assessment of problematic situations. Most people might assure the king of their ability to accomplish whatever he wanted, regardless of their competence or experience, but I did not want to misrepresent my capabilities with him, of all people."[62] Therefore, Lisa was honest with him from the very beginning.

The rest of the afternoon passed in a whirlwind. Lisa met the king's three youngest children and was given a tour of the king's stables, which were a great source of pride as he

King Hussein romanced the young Lisa Halaby with a whirlwind courtship. They spent nearly every day together, roaming the palace grounds, playing with his children, and talking into the night. After three weeks, Hussein asked to speak with Lisa's father to ask for her hand in marriage. Once married, Lisa would become Queen Noor of Jordan, changing her life forever.

possessed some of the finest Arabian horses in the world. As Lisa was preparing to leave, almost seven hours after she had arrived, the king insisted she drive herself home in one of his many collectible cars—with him beside her. As she drove through Amman, surrounded by the king's security escorts, the Hussein teased her about all the people in the streets who were trying to catch a glimpse of them. Unaccustomed to the attention, Lisa's shy nature directly contrasted King Hussein's open, playful personality.

Despite the significant differences in their age—Lisa was 26 and the recently widowed king was 41—a spark between them soon fanned into a strong flame. King Hussein was very much like her father: a charismatic man of broad vision who was keen about aviation and adventuresome. The king began telephoning Lisa regularly, frequently requesting that she visit Hashmiya, which she did. Yet despite the amount of time they started spending together, Lisa was careful not to let anyone, even her colleagues and friends, know about her developing romance. "I had lived in Jordan long enough to know that his every word, every move, every personal encounter was constantly analyzed and often misinterpreted or exaggerated."[63] Despite knowing him for such a short time, Lisa already deeply respected King Hussein and wanted to protect him from vicious rumors and hearsay that would have kept Amman's gossip circles buzzing for a long time.

Furthermore, rumors that the king was a playboy already ran rampant in Amman, and Lisa had no intention of becoming merely another royal fling. Her own father warned her against pursuing the relationship too quickly. "I like King Hussein very much, as you know," he told her, "but I don't want you to be hurt."[64] Najeeb was concerned because Lisa was spending more and more time with the king. They spent almost every evening together at Hashmiya, reading to his children, putting them to bed, and watching television.

In April 1978, after three weeks of spending nearly every moment together with Lisa, King Hussein quietly told her, "I want to see your father."[65]

Everything in Lisa's life was about to change.

4

Jordan's
New Queen
1978

The Hashemite kingdom of Jordan, a country Lisa would soon find herself ruling alongside the king, has a unique culture shaped by a volatile, captivating history. Indeed, Jordan is a nation that is ancient in some ways, but startlingly modern in others. It is a country influenced both by eastern traditions and western styles.

Before World War II, Jordan was a large tract of land stretching from the Mediterranean Sea (modern-day Israel and the Palestinian West Bank and Gaza Strip) across the desert and continuing across the desert area that borders on modern-day Iraq. Ruled by the Ottoman Empire for hundreds of years, its people were mostly village dwellers and tribes of Bedouins who traveled across the land. In 1920, the area fell under British mandate after the defeat of the

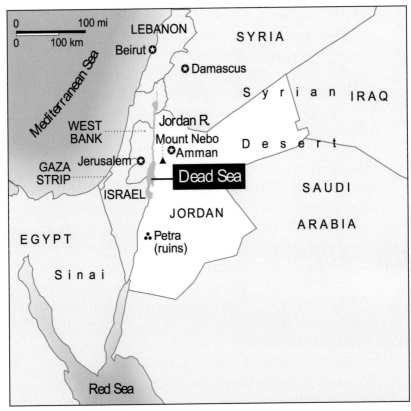

Once part of the Ottoman Empire, Jordan was freed from Turkish control by British and Allied powers during World War II. The British later named King Hussein's grandfather, Abdullah, king of Jordan, though the land granted him in return for his help in fighting the Turks was substantially smaller than promised. Bordered by Syria, Iraq, Saudi Arabia, and Israel, Jordan continues to occupy a strategic position in the volatile Middle East.

Ottomans by the British and the Allied powers during World War I.

In 1921, the British made Abdullah, the son of the famous Arab leader Sharif Hussein and the grandfather of King Hussein, the king of Jordan. Abdullah had originally been promised a much larger kingdom in exchange for helping the British defeat the Ottoman Turks. He, his father, and his brother Faisal, had done so, fighting valiantly alongside the renowned British military leader, Lawrence of Arabia, to end Ottoman rule in the Arab world. In return, the British promised to make Sharif Hussein and his sons, Abdullah and Faisal, leaders of a Hashemite kingdom that would stretch across the entire Middle East, thus making the Arab world independent from colonial rule.

However, Abdullah had to settle for another deal when Winston Churchill, the British prime minister at the time, decided that the British themselves would rule Iraq. Furthermore, the British government had also promised Jewish Zionist leaders a national homeland for the Jewish people. They were ultimately given the land west of the Jordan River, which was commonly known as Palestine and which was occupied by Palestinian Arabs. Abdullah was eventually given the land east of the river, which the British renamed Transjordania, meaning "across the Jordan." [66]

Despite being declared king, Abdullah soon realized he was not an autonomous leader. The British government sent him numerous advisors and councilors, and expected the new king to heed their advice on foreign and domestic affairs. This interference only agitated the new king, who was still raw from the betrayal he felt he had suffered at the hands of the British. Having been promised the independence of the entire Arab world, he had, instead, been given only a small country that was mostly rock and desert. Indeed, only five percent of the country is currently farmable. [67]

Regardless of the numerous setbacks, Abdullah managed to mold Jordan into a distinguished nation. He worked on modernizing the country's health systems, its roads, and its communications networks. However, Jordan's history would always be affected by what was happening on the opposite banks of the river.

The building of a national homeland for Jews was not proceeding as smoothly as had been hoped, mainly because the British found themselves unable to reconcile the conflicts their disorganization had caused. Essentially, the British had promised the same tract of land—the land known as Palestine—to both the Palestinian Arabs and the European Jews. Riots, protests, and even murders plagued the sliver of land that hugged the Mediterranean coast, making the British regret their involvement in the region in the first place.

World War II erupted as Hitler and the German Nazi regime attempted to conquer most of Europe. The British, along with the French and the Americans, fought hard to defeat the strong armies of Germany, Italy, and Japan. When the war ended, the Allied powers once again emerged victorious. After Hitler's defeat, the world soon learned the horrors that had been taking place in Germany, Poland, and other parts of Europe—specifically the nightmare of the Holocaust. Sympathy for Jews, who had endured unimaginable persecution, spread quickly, jumpstarting more dialogue on the need for a Jewish homeland in Palestine.

In 1947, the British government left Palestine, leaving its fate to the newly formed United Nations, which decided to divide the land among the Palestinian Arabs and the Jews. Despite the fact that the vast majority of people living on the land were Arabs, most of the land was given to the Jews who were emigrating from Europe. This sparked Arab fury not only in Palestine but across the Middle East. In Jordan, King Abdullah declared, "I will have the pleasure and honor to save Palestine."[68] When the state of Israel was proclaimed on May 14, 1948, war erupted the next day, with Jordan emerging as the leading force within the Arab coalition.

When the smoke cleared almost one year later, Israel had won and thousands of Palestinian Arabs were left homeless. Many of them poured into Jordan, which, as part of the armistice, was given control of the West Bank. The territory was formally annexed by Jordan in 1950. However, due to the Israeli occupation of Arab lands they had conquered in the war, the Palestinian Arabs now had less land than what they had been previously granted by the United Nations.

On July 20, 1951, two years after the war's end, King Abdullah arrived in Jerusalem with his grandson, Prince Hussein bin Talal, to perform his Friday prayers at the holy sites. A Palestinian gunman, who felt the Jordanian king had double-crossed the Palestinians in the war, fired at both Abdullah and the 14-year-old Hussein. While Abdullah was struck and killed, "Miraculously, the bullet meant for Hussein deflected off a medal he was wearing, thereby saving his life."[69] Abdullah's son Talal, Hussein's father, was declared king, but ruled only for a short period of time before he was removed from power because of mental illness. The young Hussein was only sixteen and could not assume the throne until he was eighteen: "A regency council performed his functions until he came of age and assumed his constitutional powers on May 2, 1953. The smoothness with which the reins of power were transferred through Abdullah, Talal, and Hussein was remarkable, indicating the extent to which King Abdullah had succeeded in putting the Jordanian monarchy in constitutional order."[70]

THE GOVERNMENT OF HUSSEIN

When he became king of Jordan in May of 1953, Hussein was hardly a raw, naïve eighteen-year-old. He had been trained for years to assume the throne and the position of Jordan's monarch. His grandfather Abdullah "had taken a special interest in his eldest grandson, including supervising his private tuition and subsidizing his education at Victoria College in Alexandria."[71] Furthermore, adds historian Robert Satloff, "The young prince . . . was often at his grandfather's side, acting as unofficial aide-de-camp or court interpreter."[72] However, that training would not prevent or even hinder the immeasurable challenges and dangers Hussein would face during his reign.

Despite the fact that it has a monarch, Jordan also has a parliament and a council of ministers that helps the king run the affairs of the government. The prime minister, according to Jordan's 1952 constitution, is selected by the king himself.[73] When Hussein returned from England, having completed his studies and ready to assume power, he surprised many with his political acumen. One of his first acts as king was to ask for the resignation of a prime minister who was clearly opposed to Hussein's vision for the future of his country. Satloff writes that "the king was beginning to display more than a passing restlessness with advisers that belonged more to his grandfather's generation than his own."[74] Alexander Bligh, who also wrote about the political legacy of the king, briefly notes the events and describes "an anti-Hashemite prime minister [who used] the Jordanian constitution and its freedom of party activity to try to operate against Hussein" in the years following Hussein's succession to the throne.[75] Other challenges to Hussein's throne came from Jordanians who supported the ideas of President Gamal Abdel Nasser of Egypt. Nasser preached Arab nationalism and was ideologically opposed to monarchies in the Arab world.

Hussein successfully resisted these threats against his throne, showing that he was becoming a monarch of strength and resolve. Having been educated abroad, he saw the potential for building bridges between his country and Western nations, especially with France, England, and the United States. These powers needed to see signs of stability in Jordan before committing themselves to invest time and money in Jordan's affairs. Unfortunately, stability did not come easily to the Arab kingdom. One of the most difficult issues the young King Hussein had to confront was the Palestinian-Israeli conflict. As the Palestinian West Bank of the Jordan River had been annexed by King Abdullah and fell under Jordanian rule, Hussein became heavily involved with Palestinian aspirations for an independent, autonomous country. Furthermore, as a result of the conflict with Israel, many Palestinians had been forced to flee their homes. They ended up in Jordan, either as refugees or as expatriates. Before long, problems arose.

The origins of these problems can be traced to 1948, when Palestinians first began an exodus to Jordan. "The Palestinians, all of whom were offered Jordanian nationality, tended to be more westernized and politically articulate than the Transjordanians over whom Abdullah had long ruled as a father figure," writes historian Arthur Goldschmidt.[76] The situation did not improve when Hussein became king. In fact, it worsened. By 1964, Hussein had to deal with *fedayeen*, or Palestinian militia, who were training and operating on Jordanian soil to overthrow Israeli rule of their land. The Palestine Liberation Organization (PLO) had focused on Jordan as its unofficial headquarters, and the PLO's activities directly challenged Hussein's rule of Jordan many times. However, when the 1967 war between Israel and the Arab nations erupted, Hussein joined the Arab alliance against Israel to liberate the Palestinian lands. The war lasted less than a week, but in that time, Jordan suffered 6,000 casualties and the loss of all the Palestinian land it had annexed, including the entire West Bank.[77] The military loss shocked the Arab world, which had counted on the defeat of Israel. The PLO intensified its guerrilla actions against Israel, determined more than ever to regain the land that had been taken from the Palestinians. Attacks against Israel were staged from Jordanian territory, making Jordan—and its king—quite vulnerable. In 1970, Hussein waged war against the PLO on his own land, in a terrible battle known as Black September. The Palestinians were rooted out and many were killed, forcing the PLO to relocate its headquarters to southern Lebanon.

The Palestinians would always view Hussein with intense suspicion in the decades to follow, particularly after the other Arab states declared in 1974 that the PLO was "the sole legitimate representative of the Palestinian people," thus implying that

Jordan no longer spoke for the Palestinians who lived west of the Jordan River.[78] Hussein briefly allied himself with the PLO leader, Yasser Arafat, but broke with Arafat politically in

1967 ARAB-ISRAELI WAR

Many consider the 1967 Arab-Israeli War to be, in addition to the 1948 war that saw the creation of the state of Israel, the single event that changed the modern Middle East. Also known as the Six-Day War, because it lasted less than a week, the crisis ended in the military seizure of the Palestinian territories of the West Bank and Gaza Strip by Israel.

In May 1967, Egypt's President Gamal Abdel-Nasser, who enjoyed great favor among Arabs for his emphasis on Arab unity and the importance of Palestinian independence, assembled his troops along the border of Egypt and Israel, in the Sinai Peninsula. Seeing this as a provocation, Israel moved its own troops into battle-ready positions. Both nations hurled threats across the tense border, until Israel initiated the war by attacking Egypt's air force on June 5. The attack decimated Egypt's air capabilities, thus handicapping Israel's mighty foe. From then on, Israel controlled the war.

Jordan and Syria joined Egypt in the battle against Israel, but there was little chance for an Arab victory. After seizing Gaza and the Sinai Peninsula, Israel also gained control of East Jerusalem, formerly under the protection of the Jordanians, and of the Golan Heights, which are a part of Syria.* The Camp David Peace Accords, signed between Israel and Egypt, saw the return of the Sinai to Egypt, but Israel has not yet returned the West Bank and the Gaza Strip to the Palestinian people, despite the passing of a United Nations Security Council Resolution (242) that calls for the return of these territories. It is hoped that the current peace process, mediated by the United States, will result in the fulfillment of that resolution.**

* "The Six Day War." Encyclopedia.com, *http://www.encyclopedia.com.*

** "UN Resolution 242." MSN Learning & Research, *http://encarta.msn.com/.*

1986, worried by the strong influence the PLO had over the Palestinians in the West Bank. However, over the years, Hussein and Arafat would form alliances and break them as they debated the best course of action to ensure Palestinian independence.

The other great issue in Hussein's life was personal. While the king could manage the affairs of the nation with wisdom and foresight, he had tremendous difficulty managing his own romantic life. He had been married three times by the time he met Lisa, divorcing his first two wives. "One paper condemned his 'typical male Arab attitude' toward women."[79] However, the king appeared finally happy in his third marriage to Queen Alia. Alia's tragic death in 1977 shocked the nation and Hussein, who seemed to recover only after he met Lisa Halaby.

A ROYAL WEDDING: 1978

When King Hussein first told Lisa that he wanted to speak with her father, she did not quite understand his meaning, but soon realized that he meant he wanted to ask her father for her hand in marriage. It was a sweet, traditional gesture, but it was also one more symbol of how different life was in Jordan and the types of changes to which Lisa would have to become accustomed. Lisa wondered if he had thought carefully through his proposal—had he seriously considered the implications of marrying an American woman? After all, tensions between East and West (and the United States was slowly replacing England as the greatest Western superpower), were at a fever pitch in 1978. In Iran, Islamic fundamentalism was gaining in strength and power, and rising up against Shah Mohammad Reza Pahlavi, who would be deposed in early 1979.[80] In November 1977, Anwar Sadat, the Egyptian president, had visited Israel and addressed the Israeli Knesset (Israel's parliament), offering the Israelis peace. Sadat was the first Arab leader ever to make a diplomatic visit to the new state.[81] Other Arab leaders, including Palestinian leader Yasser Arafat and Libya's President Moammar Qaddafi, labeled him a traitor.[82]

Sadat, furthermore, was supported by the Americans, and thus was seen as catering to the Western power at he expense of the Arabs. Anti-American sentiment was running high, as more Arabs became angered by what they considered to be America's narrow foreign policy.

Lisa also worried about the way in which the media would receive the marriage, especially since Queen Alia had been extremely popular. "It concerned me that I had not spent that much time talking to King Hussein about my life before Jordan. I knew how the international media could pick apart public figures. And I wanted Hussein to be wise about his choice."[83] Lisa understood that the wife of a Jordanian king (who was, no less, a direct descendent of the Prophet Muhammad, of the Hashemite tribe) would be expected to be beyond reproach. She feared that past events in her life would be twisted and misinterpreted and used against her because of the conservative atmosphere and culture of Jordan, which differed starkly from the liberal 1970s in America. She felt she had to divulge every detail to him, to give him time to ponder before they both made a commitment, but Hussein said frankly, "I really do not want to know."[84]

And yet, Lisa still worried about whether she possessed the substance of a good queen, a stateswoman. "I had lived an independent life, traveled in many different countries. I had a free, open spirit. Would I have the self-discipline necessary to make a good wife for a king?" She wondered.[85] Furthermore, Hussein already had eight children, and she would be their stepmother. Her marriage would be completely nontraditional and would bring significant changes. She would move permanently to Jordan, give up her job and her aspirations of a career in journalism, learn Arabic (which is a very difficult language to learn), and adopt Islam as her religion.

Despite all her concerns, when the king broached the subject again, asking if he could speak to her father, she took a risk and said, "Yes."

When the king called Najeeb Halaby, his friend and business associate, to ask for Lisa's hand in marriage, a stunned Najeeb blurted out, "I thought it was just for lunch."[86] He was not the first to be so surprised. Lisa herself was stunned by how

THE WIVES OF KING HUSSEIN

Queen Noor was not King Hussein's first wife. Indeed, the king had been married three times before he was wed to the woman who would be by his side until his death. King Hussein's many marriages have led some to speculate that the king viewed women as disposable commodities, but his enduring love for his last two wives suggests otherwise.

King Hussein first married a year after he ascended the throne at the age of 19. His wife, Dina bint Abdul-Hamid, was a distant cousin who had been born in Egypt. Seven years the king's senior, Queen Dina graduated from Cambridge University in England and had been a lecturer of English literature at Cairo University. They had one child together, Princess Alia, for whom Jordan's Alia Airlines would be named. A year after their wedding, the queen traveled out of the country and received word from the king that their marriage was over. Princess Alia remained with her father. The queen was demoted to the title of "Princess Dina" after the divorce. She would become an Egyptian citizen and marry a high-ranking official in the Palestinian Liberation Organization.

King Hussein's next wife was the beautiful Englishwoman Antoinette (Toni) Avril Gardiner. Gardiner was the daughter of a British army officer who had served as a mentor to Hussein. After his apparently loveless marriage to Queen Dina, the king, very much in love, gave his new wife the name "Muna," an Arabic word meaning "desire" when she converted to Islam and became Jordan's new queen in 1961. King Hussein and Queen Muna had four children together: Prince Abdullah (who would become king after his father's death), Prince Feisal, Princess Zein, and Princess Aisha. The couple divorced in 1972.

suddenly things changed—much faster than she had ever expected. She never again returned to her apartment, nor to her office, and security cars followed her everywhere. The fact was that she was the fiancee of the king; the media was

Shortly after the king divorced Queen Muna, he attended a wedding at which he ran into Alia Toukan, the daughter of an ambassador whose home the king had regularly stayed at when he attended school in Cairo, Egypt. Alia Toukan was a pretty and well educated woman. She had lived in countries all over the world because of her father's job, including Italy and the United States, and knew several languages. She had aspirations to be a diplomat, like her father, and studied political science at Hunter College. Alia began working on a project for the crown after she became reacquainted with the king, and the pair soon fell in love. They married the same year of Hussein's divorce from Queen Muna, 1972.

Queen Alia was of Palestinian origin, like many in Jordan, and she was beloved by its people. She saw a more traditional role for herself as queen, and preferred to stay out of the spotlight. Queen Alia took up many charitable causes and was the first to develop the idea for the Jerash festival that Queen Noor later made a reality. King Hussein and Queen Alia would have two biological children, Princess Haya and Prince Ali. Queen Alia also adopted a daughter, Abir Muhaisin, an infant whose family had been killed when a Soviet plane crashed into their house near the airport. It was on a return trip from visiting a hospital desperately in need of improvements that the helicopter carrying Queen Alia ran into terrible weather and crashed, killing Hussein's adored wife.

A year later, King Hussein would take notice of the young and beautiful Lisa Halaby and wed for the final time.

obsessed with her and potential danger was suddenly a factor to be seriously considered. There had been, over the years, numerous attempts on King Hussein's life, and anyone trying to hurt him might try to do so by harming his future bride.[87]

Lisa began intensive Arabic lessons, more rigorous than the ones she had been taking upon first moving to Jordan for work reasons.[88] She also began studying Islam and planned to convert, not at the king's behest but because she herself had taken an interest in the religion. It was not mandatory that the Jordanian king's wife be a Muslim, but the monotheistic faith which had sprung up in the Arabian desert centuries before and transformed the world had always attracted Lisa, who had been intrigued by it since her initial visit to Tehran a few years earlier. Though she had grown up a Protestant Christian, she had never felt fully involved in her religion, and Islam appealed to her on many levels, as she explained later:

> I admired Islam's emphasis on a believer's direct relationship with God, the fundamental equality of rights of all men and women, and the reverence for the Prophet Muhammad as well as all the Prophets and messengers who came before him, since Adam, to Abraham, Moses, Jesus, and many others. Islam calls for fairness, tolerance and charity . . . I was attracted, too, by its simplicity and call for justice. Islam is a very personal belief system.[89]

Lisa also knew that Islam was a deeply misunderstood religion in the West, in Europe and especially in her native United States, and she realized that she would have to explain her new religion to many old friends and acquaintances. In the days before her wedding, she studied and read books on Islam as well as on Jordan, its politics and history. These days were also spent with Hussein and his three youngest children, Ali, Haya, and Abir.

It was also during this time that Lisa received what she calls "the most precious gift the king ever gave me." Hussein changed her name from "Lisa" to "Noor," which means "light" in Arabic. "My name would be Noor Al Hussein, the 'Light of Hussein.' Over the next few weeks and months, a transition gradually took place in my mind, in my dreams. I became Noor."[90]

Many said the king chose the name "Noor" as an allusion to her bright blonde hair, so rare for an Arab woman. Indeed, Noor had inherited her looks from her mother's side of the family, the Carlquists, who claimed Swedish descent. It is also understandable that Noor was indeed a light in his life, which had been recently marked by darkness—the tragic death of Queen Alia and the tensions of the Middle East conflict following the 1973 war between the Arab states and Israel. Noor brought joy to his formerly dismal days.

Noor and Hussein were married on June 15, 1978, in a ceremony that fell far below royal expectations. It was a small and intensely private affair.[91] Noor wanted it to be so, as she felt uncomfortable with typical Middle Eastern wedding receptions, which can often be lavish and expensive. "Like many women of my generation," she wrote, "I always thought I would be married barefoot on a mountaintop or in a field of daisies."[92]

During the traditionally simple religious ceremony, Noor wore a simple, white wedding dress and low-heeled shoes. Two inches taller than Hussein, the willowy Noor did not want to make the difference in their heights too stark of a contrast.[93] The wedding itself took place at Zahran Palace, where Hussein's mother, Queen Zein, lived. Noor joined Hussein in the Palace's ornate sitting room for the ceremony. There were no bridesmaids, no aisle to walk down, no ritualistic event. A typical Muslim wedding, it was simple and straightforward.

In Muslim weddings, marriages are presided over by a sheik, who witnesses the couple's agreement to marry. Usually, a woman does not attend the ceremony, but has a male relative

Lisa Halaby converted to Islam and took the Arab name "Noor" on her wedding day. She and King Hussein were married in a small, private ceremony on June 15, 1978. Queen Noor insisted on attending her own wedding, which was a controversial decision as Muslim women are traditionally represented by male family members in the wedding ceremony. Noor's first act of independence was an early indicator of the progressive attitude she would hold throughout her reign.

represent her. Noor, however, had insisted on being present, and indeed, was the first woman to attend her own wedding ceremony in the history of the Hashemite family.[94] It was the first tradition with which she would break during her marriage, and she would face heavy criticism for it. [95] Though they wanted the ceremony to be private, Hussein and Noor still had an obligation to the people of Jordan, so the sitting room was filled with male members of Hussein's family, as well as scores of Arab and world media reporters and camera crews. A camera-shy Noor exchanged vows with Hussein, saying in Arabic, "I have betrothed myself to thee in marriage for the dowry agreed upon." [96] They held each other's hands as the sheik blessed the union and recited verses from the Holy Qur'an, and in less than a few minutes, the marriage was official. Hussein had a new bride, and Jordan had a new queen.

Upon returning from her honeymoon, which had opened Noor's eyes to just how different—and difficult—her new life would be, she set about the business of settling into her home in Amman. She and Hussein lived in the Hashimya Palace for some time, but the house was undergoing extensive renovation and the royal couple, as well as the three youngest children, were inconvenienced by the sound of jackhammers and other construction annoyances. [97] The royal family moved from place to place, eventually settling into a home that Noor herself would help design. The new abode would be dubbed Bab al-Salam, the "Gate of Peace."

5

Adjusting to
the Throne
1978–1986

Noor's first year as Jordan's new queen (a title she shared with King Hussein's mother) was met with difficulties far more strenuous than finding a suitable home. Indeed, it seemed that the world had a mixed reaction to her. In her memoir, Noor claims that "there was no Arab outcry, as far as I knew, about our marriage, nor any I was aware of from Jordanians. As a Halaby, I was considered an Arab returning home rather than a foreigner."[98] Furthermore, none of Hussein's previous three wives had been born in Jordan, and Queen Muna (born Toni Gardiner) was of British descent; also, Prince Hassan, the younger brother of the King, was married to a woman of Pakistani descent. Indeed, foreign brides in the royal family were probably more the norm than the exception.[99]

However, Noor was not greeted universally with open arms in her new country. Jordanians seemed suspicious of their new monarch, even though she was part Arab. Noor had formally converted to Islam on the morning of her wedding.[100] The religious sector in Jordan felt she had adopted Islam for the sake of convenience. Several reports claim that Jordanians were dissatisfied with her on numerous levels, including her "wedding-eve embrace of Islam."[101] Other charges followed, one after the other, during that first year, as noted by *People* magazine:

> The queen's stock rose little during the early years of the couple's marriage, when her increasingly high profile— she involved herself in helping the country's poor and bettering the lot of its women—prompted charges that she was too ambitious. (Being spotted at a jewelry store while her husband was abroad seeking aid from other Arab countries—'A king begs, a queen shops,' read the headline in a Kuwait newspaper—didn't help.)[102]

One biography of the queen says frankly, "In the eyes of her newfound country people, Queen Noor could do nothing right."[103]

Vilified as a spendthrift and a foreigner in some Jordanian circles, Noor was hailed as a veritable heroine in her native United States, where Americans were almost obsessed with royalty. As one writer noted, "There were frequent references in the press to another U.S. blonde who'd made a royal match, Princess Grace of Monaco. Queen Noor, however, was said to be annoyed by the comparison, and she made it clear in several interviews that she was not living a fairy-tale existence."[104] Grace Kelly, an American actress, had married Prince Rainier of Monaco, a small resort island in the south of France, and gave up her thriving acting career when she became a princess. It is easy to see, however, why Noor would reject the association. Jordan, a country with many political, social, and

religious conflicts, could hardly be compared to a kingdom that
was essentially a large tourist attraction.

Queen of Jordan was a title of prestige, but it was also a
symbol of turmoil. It was certainly no vacation.

On September 17, 1978, Israeli Prime Minister Menachem
Begin and Egyptian President Anwar Sadat agreed to a peace
accord that would reshape the Middle East. The treaty, dubbed
the Camp David Accords because it resulted from discussions
held at Camp David in September 1978, was presided over by
American President Jimmy Carter, whom the world hailed as
the man who had accomplished the impossible—he had jump-
started the process to peace in the Middle East.

However, two crucial players in the game had been
excluded: Jordan and the PLO. The Camp David Peace Accords
essentially led to the outline of a peace treaty that would return
the land Israel had wrested from Egypt during the 1967
Arab-Israeli War, open the doors to trade and commerce, and
guarantee that neither country would attack the other.[105] What
it did not do was resolve the issue of the Palestinians, whose
land remained under Israeli occupation. In fact, neither
Jordan's king nor Palestinian leader Yasser Arafat had been
invited to participate in the discussions due to their anticipated
opposition to some of the terms. It was only one of many occasions in which King Hussein would feel slighted by Israel and
the West as a peace process was crafted over the years. Furthermore, many Arabs felt that Sadat had acceded to everything the
Israelis demanded without pushing for a just resolution to the
dilemma of the Palestinian people. Millions of Palestinians
were living in exile while millions more were living in the West
Bank and Gaza Strip, now occupied by the Israeli military.

Two months after the signing of the Camp David Accords,
Hussein flew to Baghdad, where the other Arab leaders of the
Arab League member countries were participating in a summit
to review the implications of Egypt's peace treaty with Israel
for the region. The Arab League condemned the accords for

failing to address many of the region's real problems. Despite the opposition, Sadat proceeded. On March 26, 1979, the accords were signed in Washington, D.C. The United States tried to persuade Hussein, by far the most westernized and liberal of the Arab leaders, to support the accords, but he could not. As Noor writes, his reluctance stemmed from what he perceived as "Sadat's opportunism" and "the shortsightedness of the United States."[106]

STARTING A FAMILY: 1980

In the midst of all the troubles, Noor discovered that she and Hussein were expecting their first child. The couple was thrilled and looking forward to having a baby, despite a household already filled with children. However, while in England, Noor, who was in her fifth month of pregnancy, suddenly felt ill during a lunch with the king and queen of Greece. She nearly collapsed, and a doctor was quickly called in. When she began to hemorrhage, it became clear that Noor was suffering a miscarriage.

Hussein had flown to Baghdad for more talks about Sadat's accord with Israel, but he planned to return to Noor's side upon hearing the sad news. Noor insisted, however, that he remain in Baghdad: "Stay there and do what you have to do. I will be fine."[107] Though he flew to London immediately after the summit, Noor endured the trauma of the miscarriage alone, and was later plagued by voracious, seemingly heartless media coverage of her loss.[108] It seemed a queen could have anything in the world, except a little privacy.

Within a few months, Noor was pregnant again, and a son, Prince Hamzah, was born on March 29, 1980. The child was named after a Hashemite ancestor of King Hussein, an uncle of the Prophet Muhammad and a member of the Hashemite tribe. Prince Hamzah brought joy to Noor and Hussein, and Noor's stepchildren were excited about having a new baby brother in the house. Noor, who had never considered herself as possessing

The family into which Queen Noor married was already large before the addition of her and King Hussein's four children. Noor managed to be the matriarch of a family of over ten children, including Princess Aisha (left), Prince Hashim (middle) and Prince Feisal (third from right) in the top row, Prince Hamzah and Prince Ali (seated to the left and right of the king and queen, respectively), Princess Alia, Princess Zein, Princess Raiyah, Princess Haya, Princess Iman, Prince Abdullah, and Miss Abir (from left to right) in the bottom row. In addition to the responsibilities of her newly acquired family, Queen Noor faced the challenge of being accepted by the Jordanian people.

a naturally maternal instinct, found herself "stunned by the intensity of my feelings of love for my firstborn child." [109]

Before Hamzah's birth, Noor had also embarked on a new career. Gone was the bright-eyed, Princeton-educated urban planner, and in her place was a determined stateswoman with a plan. Having spent a significant amount of time living in Jordan and studying the country's history and economic situation, Noor saw much room for strengthening the nation's health care system, preserving its architectural treasures, and bettering the lives of its women and children. Just as she had not let the dramatic beauty of the Hashimya Palace prevent her from seeing its structural flaws upon her first lunch date with the king, neither did Noor allow the relative novelty of her life in Jordan prevent her from understanding its weaknesses.

The health care and well being of Jordan's children was especially important to her. She fought for socioeconomic justice in her new country with the same fervor with which she had participated in civil rights activities in the United States in her youth. In 1979, she chaired the National Committee for the International Year of the Child, and aggressively "launched a national immunization campaign, children's parks, and literature programs, as well as an initiative to establish Jordan's first children's hospital."[110] Even while she was pregnant with Hamzah, her work schedule was grueling, and her insistence on traveling around the country struck fear into the heart of the royal family's obstetrician. "There were villages to visit to launch the vaccination campaign, urban planning meetings to chair in Aqaba, and conditions in Palestinian refugee camps to check on."[111] She drove herself in her own Jeep, rumbling over bumpy roads and rough, unpaved, rural paths. As a pregnant woman cruising in a Jeep, listening to Bruce Springsteen on her radio, she must have presented a rare, unusual portrait of a queen! However, time alone in her Jeep (despite the security cars that always shadowed her) was precious to Noor, who needed privacy to balance the chaotic demands on her attention.[112]

In her first couple of years as queen, Noor saw a wide "gap between rich and poor," and realized it was "growing," as she records in her memoir.[113] One way to close the gap, she knew, was by encouraging education; after all, in the United States, a core belief of the economy and country's value system is that education can help one climb the social ladder and improve one's future earning potential. Perhaps Noor was calling upon this idea, ingrained in her since childhood, when she focused on education. Jordan already possessed a strong educational core that had produced some of the finest doctors, engineers, and lawyers and other professionals in the region, but Noor wanted to build on that foundation. In 1979, Noor established the Royal Endowment for Culture and Education, an initiative that led to "the first research on the country's specific manpower needs and awards scholarships, with special emphasis on outstanding women, for graduate studies in fields vital to Jordan's future development."[114]

In 1980, she launched another idea that took firm root: the Arab Children's Congress, which gave children across the Arab world an opportunity to assemble for two weeks and participate in activities that promoted greater understanding of one another.[115] This is an especially significant initiative because Arabs are an ethnic group spread across the entire Middle East, from as far west as Morocco in North Africa and as far east as Bahrain in the Arabian Gulf. While they speak the same language, they have different concerns and face different problems and challenges. The children in this inaugural Arab Children's Congress convened in Jordan and discussed their concerns, while also learning about each other's lives and challenges. The Arab Children's Congress empowered (and still enables) Arab children to analyze their own situations and societies and to build bridges among one another to achieve greater unity for the region's future.

Noor would make a career out of building diplomatic bridges—if the relations between the United States and Jordan had become tense, especially as a result of Jordan's objection to some of the details of the Camp David Accords, she would become the bridge that connected them. In June 1980, just a few months after the birth of Hamzah, Noor and Hussein made a visit to the United States, the first time she returned to the land of her birth since becoming Jordan's queen. Though she had become immersed in her new life, she still felt a loyalty to the United States. "My heart fluttered," she wrote, ". . . when the Jordanian and American national anthems were played at the opening lawn ceremony at the White House. Both songs stirred my senses; both countries had a claim on me."[116]

This visit was a tension-filled one, however, especially since the American president, Jimmy Carter, resented the fact that Hussein had not supported the Camp David Accords. Hussein, for his part, felt shut out for objecting to the treaty's terms and did not feel he could support a treaty that helped Egypt's relationship with Israel but hurt the chances of the Palestinians for independence and diminished the prospects of the other Arab nations in the region. "The Egyptians are free to do whatever they think best, although, morally, I feel they should take into consideration the interests of the people who've suffered beside them in combat," Hussein had said, and comments like these upset President Carter.[117] During a later visit to the White House, Noor felt the tension when her own conversations with Rosalynn Carter, for whose social work Noor had tremendous respect, turned out to be stiff and formal. "I did not know whether she was just a highly reserved individual or was deliberately expressing the tension created by our different perspectives on Middle East policy. I suspected it was the latter," remembered Noor.[118] Ever the stateswoman, however, Noor maintained a pleasant, warm demeanor with the American First Lady.

Noor, who understood and agreed with her husband's point of view on how peace in the region could be achieved, felt that she might be the perfect person to translate his views to the American public. She agreed to give interviews to the American media, but whenever she attempted to speak of anything substantive—such as politics and peace—she was met with insistent questions about details of her marriage and romance with a king. America, it seemed, had not lost its obsession with royalty. The published interviews deeply disappointed Noor, because they focused on her appearance and made fairytale-like references to her marriage to Hussein. Like many women who hold positions of prestige and power, Noor had to deal with the fact that the public interested itself in superficial details rather than real issues, and Noor's great beauty only added to the drama that the media reveled in highlighting. The blonde, tall queen had captivated American minds, and Noor realized that this interest could overshadow her past achievements as well as her future potential contributions. For example, one report in *People* magazine even referred to her as a "former decorator" for Royal Jordanian Airlines in explaining how she had met the king, ignoring the fact that she had actually held an important position within the company! "It's not that I didn't understand where my novelty lay—I was the youngest queen in the world and the only American-born queen—but I hoped to be taken as a credible voice with serious matters to discuss," she said.[119]

Noor finally had a chance to do just that more than a year later, when in the winter of 1981, Georgetown University in Washington, D.C., invited her to speak at its Center for Contemporary Arab Studies. The time was especially sensitive because the Middle East had just experienced even more tumult. Ronald Reagan, a Republican, had just been elected to the White House, which altered the attitude of the United States towards the region. More significantly, fundamentalists in Egypt had assassinated Anwar Sadat, the Egyptian president who had signed the Camp David Peace Accords with Israel. On October 6, 1981, five officers from his own army killed him during a military parade; they were fundamentalists who rejected his recent crackdown on their extremist activities.[120] Here was another "queenly" lesson for Noor, who wanted to call Sadat's wife to offer her condolences. Her compassionate impulse was blocked by Hussein and others, who felt that the Egyptian media would exaggerate the details of the call and make it appear that Jordan was warming up in its attitude toward Egypt. For Noor, however, it was simply a matter of two women, the wives of Arab leaders, who feared the same thing—the assassination of their husbands at the hands of their enemies.

Noor's speech at Georgetown would be delivered to an audience of professors, diplomats, and other professionals who knew the politics of the region thoroughly, and the queen was nervous. She had delivered speeches before, even in the United States, but they had been focused on children's health, Arab society, the arts, or other topics considered "safe" for the wife of a political leader to discuss. This would be her first political speech, and she rewrote it at least twenty times, even revising it in her hotel room just a short while before delivering it. She spoke eloquently about the conflict in the region, and emphasized the plight of the Palestinian people, whose situation under Israeli military occupation was at the heart of the problems. She stated that "any solution to [the] Arab-Israeli conflict would have to be based on self-determination for the Palestinians, on respect for international law, and on repatriation or compensation for Palestinian refugees." [121] While the press later highlighted what the queen wore and how she looked, they nevertheless reported accurately on what she said. In fact, many claimed that Noor was merely Hussein's puppet, her popularity making her an effective weapon to disseminate his beliefs.[122] While Noor expected such criticism—she had, after all, done a very untraditional thing by speaking on political matters—she rejected any notion that she had been simply a mouthpiece for Hussein. She would always speak for herself.

During her time in the United States, Noor also became aware of just how misrepresented Arabs and Muslims were in the West. As an Arab-American who had returned to her Arab roots and embraced life in the Middle East, Noor realized that she could help Arabs and Americans better understand each other's values, belief systems, cultures, and lifestyles. She spent time with media executives and movie producers trying to impart the necessity of painting a more realistic image of the people of the Middle East.

MOTHERHOOD AND NATIONHOOD: 1981–1985

Noor and Hussein had another son on June 10, 1981, and they called him Hashim, the name of the ancestral head of the

Hashemite tribe to which the Prophet Muhammad and the king both belonged. The couple had a third baby, a girl born on April 24, 1983. They named her Iman, which means "faith" in Arabic.[123] Indeed, as Noor wrote in her memoir, "It was simple faith that was sustaining us in the face of the trauma and suffering of so many in the region."[124]

The Lebanese Civil War had exploded into the already tense region in 1975, when Phalange Lebanese forces—a Christian

ARABS IN THE WESTERN MEDIA

Queen Noor is especially dedicated to improving the image of Arabs and Muslims in the West. As an Arab-American who embraced an Arab nation as her adopted country, the queen is keenly aware of the lack of understanding between Americans and Arabs. This lack of understanding is especially evident when one considers how Arabs are portrayed in the American media.

During the era of silent films, one of America's most famous actors was Rudolph Valentino, best recognized for his starring role in *The Sheik,* a film about an Arab desert prince who captures an English woman and holds her against her will. Since then, Arabs in Hollywood have rarely been portrayed as anything more than villains, barbarians, and most recently, terrorists. Some of the most recent films that have outraged Arab-Americans and sparked accusations of misrepresentations of Arabs and Arab-Americans include *Rules of Engagement* (2000), *True Lies* (1994) and *Protocol* (1984) in which Arabs are depicted as terrorists and universally evil people.*

Michael Suleiman, author of *The Arabs in the Mind of America*, explains the situation. "Americans hold generally negative views of Arabs . . . Thus, in a recent survey, they [Arabs] were seen as simultaneously rich and 'backward, primitive, uncivilized' people who dressed strangely, mistreated women, and appeared to be 'warlike, bloodthirsty,' 'treacherous, cunning,' 'strong, powerful,' and 'barbaric, cruel'."** Suleiman further explains the ways in sect—attacked Palestinians in east Beirut. What ensued was a fifteen-year-long war that resulted in the deaths of over 150,000 people, as well as irreversible divisions among the various religious sects in Lebanon.[125] The conflict ensnared neighboring Syria and Israel, whose forces further ripped apart an already torn Lebanon. It was all Jordan could do to keep itself out of the war, a difficult task considering the large Palestinian population living in the Hashemite kingdom. In 1982, the situation became

which these flawed perceptions harm American relationships with the Arab world, as well as the ways in which these stereotypes result in harassment of Arabs and political tensions. Jack Shaheen, author of *Reel Bad Arabs: How Hollywood Vilifies a People*, discusses the same topic in his book, offering many examples of the stereotyping of Arabs in American popular culture.

Queen Noor worked closely with some of Hollywood's most influential players, including Jack Valenti, the president of the Motion Picture Association of America, to discuss the skewed portrayal of Arabs and Muslims in the United States and to find ways to correct those stereotypes. "It was so upsetting to be watching a very entertaining film, feeling relaxed and even laughing out loud, and suddenly freeze up whenever an Arab character would be introduced," says Noor. "These depictions bore no resemblance to the Arab people as I knew them. Where were the kind, civilized, hospitable people with whom I came into contact every day in Jordan?"*** As a result of her work and that of others, perhaps Arabs will some day be depicted more accurately in America's media.

  * "Quiz." Arab American Institute, *http://www.aaiusa.org/quiz.htm*

 ** Michael Suleiman. *The Arabs in the Mind of America*. Brattleboro, Vt.: Amana Books, 1988, p. 2.

*** Queen Noor, *Leap of Faith*, p.195–196.

even worse when Phalange militia, aided by the Israeli military, invaded the Palestinian Sabra and Shatila refugee camps in southern Lebanon, massacring thousands in an act that shocked the world and aroused international condemnation. What the massacre at Sabra and Shatila did do, however, was to reassert the importance of resolving the Arab-Israeli conflict and finding a just resolution for the displaced Palestinians.

However, the new Reagan administration in the United States had altered the traditional perspective towards Israel, taking a more favorable approach to the Jewish state at the expense of the Arab nations. The United States pressured Hussein to make a peace treaty with Israel, just as Sadat had done a few years earlier, but Hussein resisted because he felt that he could only sign a peace treaty that was a just and equitable one, not one that would become a mere bandage on the problems of the region.[126] The United States, however, felt he was missing an important opportunity for peace, and tension between the two nations mounted even higher.

During these years, Noor struggled to make time for her growing family. The royal family eventually moved into Al Nadwa in 1983, and although it would not be their final home, it sufficed for several years. The house was a simple structure, lacking any of the ornate features and décor that one would expect in the home of a king. Noor cut down on the household staff, though the couple still required some servants to handle their large family as well as all the distinguished guests and heads of state who paid them visits. As Noor recalls, "Distinguished guests—from Queen Elizabeth to the Sultan of Brunei—would sometimes pass by a jumble of tricycles, bicycles, and [baby carriages] on their way to the front door."[127] Yet, Noor sought to give her three young stepchildren, as well as her own three young ones, a natural and relaxed upbringing. She and Hussein had dinner with their children every evening if possible, and tried to spend time with them every day, but duty constantly called, and their home life was frequently interrupted by phone calls and other business. While Noor did not like the idea of relying on someone to help her raise the children, she realized that her official commitments were enormous, and she was ultimately grateful for the services of nannies and other professionals. "In the end," she wrote, "it was a combined effort. It had to be. I like to think our children did have the advantage of growing up in an environment in which the concept of dedication to something larger than themselves was simply a part of life." [128]

At the same time, Noor's own work commitments were increasing. She had opened her own office, which surprised many people within the royal court as well as throughout the country, but she needed to have a space of her own. [129] Hussein suggested that she open an office in Al Ma'Wa, a building close to where the royal court's office were housed, and a place which had been a favorite of the late King Abdullah, Hussein's grandfather. "It was the first such office for someone in my position," writes Noor, "and many in the royal court were not used to the concept of a queen who would function relatively independently from the patriarchal royal court offices, which were focused exclusively on the king. It was interesting to me that many found it impossible to imagine that I could set out my own priorities, establish projects, and speak publicly on my own initiative." [130] At the time, she wrote, her main priority was "to fill the gaps in development programs and promote international understanding at this turbulent point in Middle East history." [131]

Little could she have known just how critical the situation in the Middle East would become, and just how important a role she would play.

6

A Time of Turmoil
1986–1991

On February 9, 1986, another daughter was born to Jordan's king and queen, Noor's fourth child and Hussein's twelfth. Her name, Raiyah Al Hussein, meant the "flag" or "banner" of Hussein in Arabic.[132] Raiyah arrived, like her other siblings, during a critical juncture in the relationship between Jordan and the rest of the Middle East, at a time when her father was busy trying to negotiate peace deals and calm down a situation that seemed ready to light afire.

Despite the peace treaty with Egypt (which held fast, in spite of the assassination of Sadat), the problem between Israel and the other Arab countries, and especially between Israel and the Palestinians, threatened to overwhelm the region. Many years earlier, King Hussein had proposed the idea of an international conference on peace in the Middle East. Indeed, one of the reasons the Camp David Peace Accords had disappointed him was that the Americans, Israelis, and Egyptians had rejected his idea of international negotiations for more private and exclusive ones. In light of the continuing hostilities in the region, Hussein began advocating the idea of an international conference along the lines he had proposed years earlier.

By the mid-1980s, America and Israel had both expressed an interest in such an idea. The sticking point was the fact that the Israelis would not recognize the PLO as the representative of the Palestinian people; the PLO, however, could gain recognition by accepting the United Nations Resolution 242, which called for a separation of the land in question into two states, Israel and Palestine. Resolution 242 also mandated that the PLO recognize Israel's right to exist as a nation, without fear of harm from its neighbors, something the Palestinians, who were suffering terribly from the loss of their homeland, were reluctant to accept. The PLO leader, Yasser Arafat, refused again and again to accept UN Resolution 242, which made it impossible for the PLO to participate in Hussein's proposed international conference.[133]

Hussein spent much time in negotiations with Arafat, urging him to accept 242 and participate in the conference. Despite the hostilities that undoubtedly lingered after Black September, Arafat and Hussein both determined to see past their differences for the security of the region. Arafat, however, who had to answer to his people, refused to participate unless the end result would be an independent state for the Palestinians.[134] Hussein did not feel he could make any more progress, and he arrived at the difficult conclusion that he had to sever Jordan's relations with the PLO until a more promising relationship could be forged. This also meant suspending his goal of an international conference on peace in the region, and the succession of failures thoroughly discouraged him.[135]

Noor was keeping busy with the new baby and her other young children as well as with her many official activities. She eventually combined all her responsibilities under one unit, the Noor Al Hussein Foundation, to make her commitments more manageable.[136] However, it was becoming increasingly difficult to manage a household with twelve children, especially when the older children were experiencing typical "growing pains."[137] She felt that they resented her for almost everything and that they even used her as a "family scapegoat."[138] The unhappiness the older children were experiencing was blamed almost solely on their stepmother, and the children compounded the problem by involving other family members, whose input only complicated matters. Because Hussein was occupied with national and international matters, Noor was usually left to try to handle the disputes by herself, but she became so discouraged that she felt "completely helpless, responsible, and very alone."[139] On occasion, she was even driven to ponder whether her marriage could survive in the face of such anger on the part of her eight stepchildren.

Luckily, she had many activities to keep her occupied and her thoughts otherwise absorbed. In 1981, she had seen one of her most lasting achievements come to fruition: the annual Jerash Festival, which brings an assembly of artists, performers, and musicians from around the world to Jerash, an ancient city whose ruins date back to the Greco-Roman era. The Jerash Festival was a brilliant public relations move, one that revitalized Jordan's suffering economy as it attracted people from all over the Middle East and the world to witness the showcase of talent that took to the stage each year.[140] However, even this tremendous success of Noor's was slamming into obstacles during this low point in her life: radical fundamentalists deemed the popular festival "un-Islamic" and suggested that it promoted anti-Arab and anti-Muslim values.[141]

Furthermore, a declining economy in Jordan had sparked frustration and anger in the streets of Jordanian cities; riots broke out in April 1989, while the royal couple were on a state visit to Washington, D.C.[142] The rioters, infuriated by the

Queen Noor soon saw areas where she could be of service to Jordan's people. Her tireless efforts have brought enhanced education and improved healthcare to Jordan's children. She has also helped to promote cultural and artistic growth in the nation, founding the Jerash Festival—an international celebration of art, culture, performance, and music held each year in the ancient Greco-Roman city for which it is named.

government's price hike on fuel, irrigation water, electricity, telephone services, and other necessities, caused much destruction and damage, especially to health clinics, for which Noor had worked so tirelessly to find funding and support. In the furor, rumors about Noor herself circulated aggressively. The gossip portrayed Noor as a spendthrift who bought jewels and expensive clothes at obscene prices. The rumors gained momentum, and one in particular "snowballed from my alleged purchase of a ring for $5,000 to buying that same ring for $1 million, then ballooned from a ring to a brooch to a necklace to a whole suite of jewelry for $20 million! Whoever was responsible for the rumor even circulated a supposed photocopy of the check I had written to the jeweler."[143] These rumors were especially harsh because they exploited the economic straits Jordan as a whole was facing and turned the queen into a scapegoat upon whom people could heap their fury and complaints. While her next visit to meet with Jordanian citizens was cordial and she received her usual warm welcome, the queen was still bothered by the fact that such horrible gossip could be believed by people.[144]

The riots of April were eventually settled by the king. Upon his return from Washington, he imposed martial law until calm was established, and then he pushed through several democratic reforms to the government's structure. The people of Jordan accepted the suggested changes and peace was restored.[145]

And then, a war exploded close to home.

THE GULF WAR: 1991

After Queen Noor visited Iraq in the spring of 1989, she reflected upon what she had seen. "For the Iraqi people to have no other choice but to focus all their dreams and hopes on a single person seemed to me to represent an unsustainable future for the country." That "single person" around whom she had witnessed "a cult of personality" developing was President Saddam Hussein.[146]

During a visit to the National Art Gallery, she noticed that most of the artwork was dedicated to the Iraqi president; like-wise, a kindergarten classroom was the platform for teaching Iraqi children almost to worship the leader. Indeed, Noor wrote that the idolization building up around Saddam Hussein reminded her of "German World War II propaganda."[147]

Over the next several months, King Hussein and Queen Noor found Saddam Hussein's behavior increasingly alarming. The Iraqi president, who had engaged in an eight-year-long war with his neighbor Iran in order to prevent the religious fundamentalism of Iran from spreading into Iraq, had begun to speak out more forcefully against the United States and Israel. Furthermore, he focused his verbal attacks against Kuwait, Jordan's Arab neighbor to the south, charging the small gulf state with drilling across the Iraqi border and stealing Iraqi oil. He also charged Kuwait with producing oil beyond what OPEC, the Organization of the Petroleum Exporting Countries, deemed suitable, accusing the country of selling oil more cheaply than Iraq could afford to sell it.[148] His rhetoric against Kuwait prompted King Hussein of Jordan to try to intervene to maintain the peace of the region; the worried king also telephoned American President George H.W. Bush as well as the British ambassador to Jordan to alert them of the predicament. "Inexplicably," wrote Queen Noor, neither man "seemed particularly interested."[149] After a meeting between Iraqi and Kuwaiti officials failed to improve the situation, King Hussein confessed to Noor that he felt "terribly nervous for the first time."[150] He had reason to feel such anxiety, since an attack on an Arab country by another Arab country would be an unprecedented move in recent history, one from which the region and the notion of "Arab unity" would never recover. Furthermore, Kuwait and Iraq were neighbors of Jordan, and many Jordanians, especially those of Palestinian origin, felt sympathetic to Saddam Hussein because of his verbal attacks against Israeli policies toward the Palestinian people.[151]

On August 2, 1990, Iraqi forces, which had been massing on the border of Kuwait, invaded their much smaller neighbor, defeating its army within a matter of days.[152] The world was stunned by the invasion of Kuwait, and Jordan was, as Hussein and Noor had known, drawn quickly into the matter, especially when the United States began discussing its own plans to attack Iraq to liberate Kuwait. Hussein was hesitant to condemn his neighbor and wanted to pursue negotiation. However, the new American president, George H.W. Bush, with whom Hussein and Noor had a friendly, warm relationship, was convinced that attacking Iraq was the only feasible resolution.

Iraq's invasion of Kuwait had taken place on the same day as Queen Zein's birthday, and Noor had been with her mother-in-law while the news of the attack unfolded. The two women, both astute and politically knowledgeable, understood that King Hussein's reluctance to condemn Iraq would be viewed harshly by the United States and its Western allies. They also understood that Noor herself could play an important role in communicating the king's position to the West. "Queen Zein urged me to take an active role in defending Jordan's position, especially in the United States," wrote Noor. "It would be the one time she strongly encouraged me to assume such an untraditional role. Neither of us could have had any idea how intense the pressure would become." [153]

During the days and weeks in which the United States built up international support for an attack on Iraq, Jordan felt bypassed and neglected, especially when King Hussein was

THE GULF WAR

The period of 1990–1991 was an especially difficult one in the history of Jordan, as the economically weak Hashemite kingdom was politically pulled into both the Iraqi invasion of Kuwait and the ensuing U.S.-led war on Iraq.

The border between Kuwait and Iraq had always been a tense one. Iraq, an oil-wealthy nation, has long considered Kuwait a former province of its country and, in 1990, sought to regain it. Kuwait, which also has an oil-dependent economy, lies on the Persian Gulf and has an expansive shoreline, thus enjoying easy access to trading and commerce. Iraq, in justifying an invasion of Kuwait, accused Kuwait of drilling across the border into Iraqi oil fields. Yet another Iraqi claim insisted that Kuwait should forgive the debt owed to it by Iraq, which had just recently emerged from the costly, ten-year Iran-Iraq war and needed the money to rebuild its infrastructure.

Tensions continued to escalate until August 1990, when Iraqi troops crossed the border, occupying Kuwait within days. Most of the international community, including the other members of the Arab repeatedly cut out of the discussions on the crisis.[154] Hussein fielded several personal attacks on himself, and he was repeatedly discouraged while trying to avert war in the region. He became so discouraged, in fact, that, according to Noor, he seriously considered abdicating his throne or passing the crown on to a successor who would normally only succeed to the throne upon Hussein's death. It was a critical moment for Jordan as the United States and others understood neither Hussein's reluctance to condemn Iraq, nor his eagerness to continue seeking a peaceful solution rather than supporting a military resolution to Kuwait's liberation.

Jordan was in a difficult position, as a war with Iraq meant that refugees would overwhelm the borders of the already

League, condemned the invasion. One exception was neighboring Jordan, because King Hussein did not want his country to be drawn into taking sides in the conflict. Thus, Jordan remained politically silent, even though it absorbed millions of refugees from both Iraq and Kuwait. When the United States led its own attack on Iraq in January 1991, Jordan suffered even further, taking in so many refugees that its own borders seemed ready to burst. The burden placed tremendous pressure on Jordan's already weak economy.

The war ended with the defeat of the Iraqi army, although President Saddam Hussein remained in power. The United Nations also imposed strict economic and military sanctions on Iraq, which served to isolate the country from the rest of the world and to severely reduce its capabilities to serve its population. The sanctions lasted more than ten years and nearly crippled Iraq, but were lifted at the end of the recent Gulf War, which has led to the political demise of President Saddam Hussein.*

* "Persian Gulf War." MSN Learning & Research,
  http://encarta.msn.com/encnet/refpages/RefArticle.aspx?refid=761551555.

economically struggling kingdom. Refugees from Kuwait—
Asians, Moroccans, Pakistanis, Somalis, and people of many
other nationalities and ethnic groups—had already poured into
Jordan seeking escape from the Iraqi invasion. "We had no tents
or blankets for them at first," said Noor, who kept a careful eye
on the support given to the refugees, "and the ground was very
rough, but every night 10,000 more evacuees would arrive." [155]
In fact, Jordan, a country of less than 3.5 million people, had
absorbed 3 million more during the crisis. [156] Noor spent most of
her time at the border, monitoring the situation and deciding how
best to handle it. She also designed creative solutions to many of
the problems facing the refugees; for example, many of them were
foreign workers who had been working in Kuwait or Iraq and
had to be returned to their own countries before winter settled
into the region. However, the International Organization for
Migration had a difficult time finding transportation for these
people, and there was no time to be spared. Noor made use of her
connections and telephoned Richard Branson, the chairman of
Virgin Atlantic Airways, to seek his help. Within days, Branson
arrived in Jordan with "a planeload of relief supplies and the very
welcome promise of continued support." [157]

The refugee issue was still threatening to harm Jordan's
economy and stretch its already strained resources. The country
was in trouble, and the situation would become even worse if a
Western attack on Iraq ensued. The situation left King Hussein
feeling very insecure and unsure of the future, but he did not
abdicate. In the end, Queen Noor and other Jordanians were
instrumental in convincing him that his country needed him in
this crisis more than ever. [158] Instead, Noor encouraged him to visit
the United States and to speak personally with President George
Bush to explain his position. The trip was not successful and was
described by Hussein's nephew Prince Talal, who accompanied
the king to Washington, as "quite a raw experience." [159] From
King Hussein's perspective, President Bush did not seem interested
in his idea of peaceful negotiations with Saddam Hussein;

neither did Margaret Thatcher, the prime minister of England, whom King Hussein visited next.[160] War seemed inevitable.

It also seemed inevitable that Noor would have to assume the leading role she had discussed with Queen Zein. One day, more than a month after Iraq's invasion of Kuwait, Noor and Hussein watched a CNN interview in which United States Senator Frank Lautenberg discussed charges that had been leveled at King Hussein. Noor defended herself and Hussein from Lautenberg's accusations:

> Lautenberg quoted President [Hosni] Mubarak of Egypt as saying that my husband had taken bribes, that he knew about Iraq's invasion of Kuwait ahead of time, and that he had supported—even been part of—the invasion of Kuwait. We decided Senator Lautenberg must have misunderstood or misinterpreted what Mubarak had said, or that the senator's comments had been taken out of context, but we were mistaken. The king went to Morocco a few days later, on September 20, and learned from the Algerian president and King Hassan of Morocco that President Mubarak was also spreading these stories to other Arab heads of state.[161]

The shock to Hussein and Noor was immense—not only did they have to defend themselves against accusations by Western leaders, but apparently also against those leveled at them by Arab leaders like Mubarak. The rumors took effect: Saudi Arabia, which was worried that Iraq would invade it next and which had allied itself with the Americans and Western powers, expelled Jordan's diplomats from its borders and cut off its oil supply to Jordan, which was heavily dependent upon it.

Noor began speaking actively on behalf of her husband and her country. While attending the Children's Summit at the United Nations a few weeks later, she encountered Suzanne Mubarak, the wife of President Hosni Mubarak, and told her pointedly that the dishonesty being perpetuated was unacceptable. Her comment put the Egyptians on the defense, and Hussein called Noor later that day to say that her comments to Mrs. Mubarak had already been circulated and that the Mubarak administration was actively justifying its claims against Jordan.[162]

Noor's encounter with President George and Mrs. Barbara Bush at the same summit was also tense and awkward. Considering that the Bushes were good friends, Noor broached the issue of the invasion of Kuwait, the threat of war by the United States and the Western powers, and the difficulty of Jordan's position—and the way it had been misrepresented—in the matter. Noor also emphasized her fears for the situation of the refugees who had been created thus far, as well as for the innocent people of Iraq who would be the victims of an attack on Saddam Hussein. The president and the First Lady, according to Queen Noor, treated her in a manner that was "particularly cool."[163] Mrs. Bush, who supported her husband's belief that the crisis could only be resolved militarily, was especially incensed with the queen. Noor later wrote, "I would continue to speak out after the war started about the humanitarian consequences of the war and the suffering of the people of Iraq, which evidently so angered Mrs. Bush that she sent a message to me through an American official that she considered me a traitor."[164] Being called a traitor could not have been easy for the queen, who still loved the country of her birth and was loyal to its ideals of freedom and justice for all. In her memoir, Noor speculates that the purpose of Mrs. Bush's message was to intimidate her into ceasing her outspokenness on the issue of the war.

Noor, however, had sparked a flame, and she realized that when she spoke, people paid attention. The causes of peace and justice now possessed a powerful voice. She continued to make the dangers of the U.S.-led coalition against Iraq a priority in her speeches and talks to various audiences during this time period, and once again, many accused her of being a puppet for her husband. Even worse, people accused the king of being a coward who used his wife to voice opinions he was afraid to voice himself.

When war broke out on January 16, 1991, with bombs from coalition forces raining down on Baghdad, Noor immediately began preparing for the consequences.[165] The refugee camps were once again filling up, and cholera broke out among the refugees. Supplies were also in demand, and the harsh winter weather was setting into the region. All of these issues kept Noor occupied. Allied planes bombed cars and oil transportation vehicles along the road that connected Amman and Baghdad, killing Iraqi as well as Jordanian civilians.[166] "Aside from Kuwait and Iraq, no country suffered more from the Gulf crisis than Jordan," the queen wrote of that dark period in her memoir.

However, despite Noor's real concerns and the challenges facing her country, she continued to be plagued by flawed news coverage, especially by the western media. *Spy* magazine ran a negative news story about her, referring to her as "Jordan's All-American Queen—Mrs. King Hussein," and *The Washington Post* ran a story claiming that she planned to flee Jordan with Hussein and had even purchased a costly, seven-acre property for herself and the king in Florida in preparation for their exile.[167] This media onslaught came at a time when the American-born queen, was working day and night to help her people, the Jordanians, who were growing increasingly furious with the United States for its leading role in the war against their neighbor, Iraq. With anti-American sentiment on the rise, Noor found herself in a precarious and dangerous position.

The King's Battle

1991–1998

The U.S.-led war on Iraq, now known as the first Gulf War, ended on March 3, 1991, with Iraq's defeat. Harsh economic and military sanctions that would last through the next decade and effectively cripple the oil-producing country were imposed. Eventually, the negative political attitudes toward Jordan also began to lessen, and the Hashemite kingdom began to re-enter the political scene. Tension between Noor and Hussein, however, had mounted. The Gulf War had brought much negative publicity for the king, despite his tireless efforts for a peaceful resolution. At the same time, Noor's work with refugees and humanitarian relief efforts had brought her praise in many circles.[168]

The strain became only more palpable when a rumor claiming that King Hussein was having an affair emerged in many circles in Amman. Having heard similar gossip that attempted to disparage her marriage many times before, Noor refused to take this particular story seriously. But when one of the king's own daughters contacted Noor (who had been out of the country) and expressed her concern, the queen finally listened. The rumor claimed dramatic and drastic things about the young woman, a Jordanian government employee. Noor heard, as she later wrote, "that my husband had met this woman's family; that he was planning to divorce me and marry her; that he had already bought her a house; that they were secretly married."[169] Apparently, Noor's time abroad had fueled the rumor even further.

As a child, Noor had witnessed her parents' marriage unravel, and it had caused her much pain. She did not want her own children to suffer emotionally in the same way. "I had lived an independent life before I married and assumed I could again, if necessary," she wrote.[170] She knew how to survive on her own and earn a living, but she hoped that the story was just another concoction of interfering gossips in Amman. To be sure, she confronted Hussein, informing him that the story was disrupting the family and requesting the truth. When he denied the gossip "with a baffled expression on his face," she knew he was being honest.[171] They faced the rumors together, deciding not to fire the woman so as not to damage her reputation and inflame the gossips even further. Despite their decision to deny allegations about the affair, the rumors spread further and further, piling even more stress onto their marriage.

It took a frightening incident for Noor and Hussein to remember how deeply their love ran. In August 1992, King Hussein suffered a cancer scare when doctors discovered an abnormal growth in his body that contained precancerous cells. Doctors removed the cells along with one of Hussein's kidneys. The operation took place at the Mayo Clinic in Minnesota in the United States, and Noor stayed with the king throughout the entire ordeal.[172] The news delivered by the doctors was positive: there did not seem to be signs of abnormality or cause for further worry. The good prognosis provided the couple with an opportunity to improve their relationship. Hussein and Noor had been growing apart because of their demanding schedules, the negative impact of the Gulf War, and the damaging rumors about their marriage. Now things changed. "The cancer scare snapped Hussein out of his depression," wrote Noor, "and he became once again the eager and engaged person he had been before the Gulf War."[173]

Negative media reports followed them nonetheless, reminding Noor that nothing at all was private in the life of royalty. Newspapers around the world printed speculative reports on the surgery performed on the king, and one Israeli newspaper, Noor recalls in her memoir, stated that the mystery illness was brain cancer. The same paper reported that the king had only six months left to live.[174]

However, the flood of sympathetic phone calls and messages from leaders around the world was so overwhelming that Noor and Hussein both felt that the event had reduced the negative impact of the Gulf War on relations between Jordan and the rest of the world. One evening, while Hussein was recovering at River House under the careful and attentive nursing of his queen, the couple was invited to the White House to have dinner with President George H.W. Bush and Mrs. Bush and Secretary of State James Baker and his wife. It was a quiet, pleasant evening, and it seemed that the earlier rift in the diplomatic relations between the two nations had been mended.[175] Hussein had also regained the support of most in his own country; more than one million people crowded the streets of Amman to welcome him home: "People were laughing, weeping, waving hand-painted signs, holding up pictures of Hussein and of the two of us, running, screaming, throwing kisses and flowers and even their bodies at the cars, trying to reach in the windows and touch him.... Over the protests of his security detail, Hussein sat on the car roof as he waved and received the embraces of his people."[176]

MONTHS IN MINNESOTA: 1993–1997

King Hussein survived this early encounter with cancer, and his energies and hope for peace in the region were renewed. Yet a new challenge lay on the horizon, something which had been brewing for many years. It was the same story of the Palestinians and the Israelis, and tensions began erupting again. The Oslo Accords, the first peace treaty between the two parties, had been signed on the White House lawn in 1993. While the peace treaty brought relief to many in the region, others, especially Arabs, were discontented by the fact that discussions and resolutions of many of the conflict's most troubling issues had been delayed. The outlined process, which was basically a "land for peace" plan, had yet to be implemented. King Hussein was one of those who believed that Arafat had agreed to give up too much and had not insisted enough on definite borders for a Palestinian state. Nonetheless, he had endorsed the peace treaty.[177] Despite the suspicions of many, the peace process began slowly and steadily, the West Bank and Gaza began developing their infrastructures and plans for independence, and the Palestinians waited for the day when the Israeli military would leave their land and end the occupation.

The peace process soon suffered a blow when Israeli Prime Minister Yitzhak Rabin, who had shaken hands with Yasser Arafat on the White House lawn after signing the Oslo Accords, was assassinated by a fundamentalist Israeli in early November 1995. Noor and Hussein attended Rabin's funeral in Jerusalem (Hussein's first visit there since 1967) and mourned a man they considered to be a brave hero, a man who had given his life for peace. Saddened by his death and what it meant for the peace process, Noor renewed her energies for peace in the region by becoming involved in various activities. These included Seeds for Peace, a program which brought together Palestinian and Israeli children to promote understanding, and United World

The assassination of Israeli Prime Minister Yitzhak Rabin in 1995 weakened hopes for peace in the Middle East. In a showing of support, King Hussein and Queen Noor traveled to Israel for the funeral. In the wake of this tragedy, Queen Noor applied herself to several projects aimed at promoting peace and tolerance in the region.

Colleges, a network of colleges that emphasizes peace and tolerance for all peoples.

Noor also revitalized her work on behalf of women during this period, focusing on helping Jordanian women empower themselves. As a woman who had worked and earned her own money, and who continued to work after her marriage, Noor believed deeply in the empowerment women attained by earning a salary. "In my experience," she wrote, "whenever women engage as equal partners with men, development and progress accelerate and endure." [178] She had encouraged the talent Jordanian women exhibited through their handiwork, and had made it a habit to wear ethnic, handmade dresses during state and public visits in order to bring visibility to the work of her countrywomen. "I have always worn them [the dresses] with great pride and delight, and over the years these dresses have also become extremely fashionable in Jordan and much sought after in other Arab states."[179] The Noor Al Hussein Foundation worked to establish the National Handicrafts Development Project, which aided women who were trying to earn their own money. It became a successful and sustainable way for women in Jordan's poorer areas to boost their income and their quality of life.

However, it was not long before King Hussein's health began failing again. He had never stopped smoking although his doctors told him that the precancerous cells they had detected were probably related to his vice. In late 1997, he began suffering from night fevers and general fatigue.[180] Several months later, shortly after his sixty-second birthday, which coincided with their twenty-year wedding anniversary, his health worsened. Hussein and Noor decided to return to the Mayo Clinic. There, doctors informed them that the king had developed cancer, non-Hodgkin's lymphoma, which had spread to several parts of his body.[181] The diagnosis was the worst news they could have expected to hear. The royal family was stunned, especially Noor, who had to be the one to inform the king's children and the rest of the family while trying to absorb the news herself. Though she masked her emotions as best as she could, acting brave for the sake of the children, she was terrified. In her memoir, Noor recalled:

> I felt such fear, such bottomless anxiety at the thought of losing my husband, my best friend, my dearest love and inspiration that it threatened to paralyze me. For twenty years we had been husband and wife, father and mother, life partners through international crises and domestic turmoil in Jordan. . . . To lose this man would be a catastrophe on every level imaginable. He simply could not die.[182]

Hussein remained at the Mayo Clinic for several months;

his hospital suite included a small kitchen, a dining room, and an adjacent room where Noor herself slept every night, determined not to let him undergo the lengthy period of treatment alone.[183] Hussein underwent intensive chemotherapy, as well as a bone marrow transplant, in a period of five months. When he was able, he took breaks to travel to River House with Noor for mental as much physical respite.[184] His children visited him frequently, staying either at a nearby hotel or meeting them at River House whenever he was there. While in Washington, during rest from chemotherapy, Noor and Hussein were invited to the White House for dinner with Bill and Hillary Clinton. As they ate hamburgers on the Truman Balcony, the four discussed politics, world affairs, and King Hussein's and President Clinton's mutual love of motorcycles.[185]

While the doctors assured Noor that there was reason to hope Hussein would survive the cancer, she refused to leave his side and even tried various folk remedies and other alternative therapies. Having heard that rubies were healing stones, she bought Hussein ruby cuff links and studs. She later wrote, "The children and I started a ritual of sorts, during which we would stand around his bed and gently touch his skin with the rubies. We were willing to try anything."[186] They were all desperate for his recovery.

PEACE FALLS APART: 1998

While Noor rarely left Hussein's side during his illness, she had many important issues to which she had to attend. For example, after the death of Diana, Princess of Wales, Noor loaned her celebrity to a very important cause. The English princess had been a major sponsor of the global effort to stop the use of landmines, which kill and maim scores of civilians around the world each year. Noor committed herself to carry on Diana's crusade against landmines. In July 1998, she hosted the first Middle East Conference on Landmines Injury and Rehabilitation in Amman. At the conference, she said:

> Mines left behind after World War Two half a century ago are still killing children in Egypt. Displaced families returning home in celebration and hope after years of war in Bosnia are torn apart without warning. When peace is declared, the guns and mortars are stilled, but no one turns off the mines. And because they are small, and destroy lives one by one, their horrific consequences go as unnoticed as the mines themselves.[187]

Her efforts to prevent the use of landmines and to convince governments to locate and disable the mines that already existed in civilian-populated areas helped draw global attention to the issue. She had already been a supporter of the International Campaign to Ban Landmines and became the patron of the Landmine Survivors Network. On October 1, 1998, the International Campaign saw a major success as the United Nations announced the fortieth ratification of the Ottawa Mine Ban Treaty, which promoted the importance of the issue and the necessity to provide more support to victims.[188]

Like his wife, King Hussein also put the affairs of the nation and the world before his own. He never stopped working while he was at the hospital, and though Noor tried to keep newspaper or magazine articles that would upset him out of his sight, he nevertheless followed events regarding the peace process, which was struggling to survive. President Clinton, who had overseen the signing of the Oslo Accords in 1993, was now meeting with Israeli Prime Minister Benjamin Netanyahu and Yasser Arafat at the Wye River Conference Center in Maryland to move the process forward. It had been stalled repeatedly due to outbreaks of violence in the region as well as by accusations by each side that the other had broken the original agreement.

HONOR KILLINGS

When she became queen, Noor began studying Jordanian culture and society, especially probing into the situation facing women. Despite western perceptions of Middle Eastern countries, women in many Arab-Muslim societies tend to live quite well. They worked in a variety of professions and contributed to society on many levels. As in any country or culture, however, some regions or elements tend to be more conservative and patriarchal than the mainstream. In Jordan, this is especially true of places that sanction "honor killings."

The term refers to murders in which a woman is killed by a family member, usually her own father or a brother, because it is discovered (or, in some cases, merely suspected) that she has been associating with men who are not part of her family or she has become pregnant out of wedlock—in short, any behavior that is considered disgraceful to her family's honor. The Jordanian constitution still technically permits honor killings: "He who discovers his wife or one of his female relatives committing adultery and kills, wounds, or injures one of them, is exempted from any penalty."[*]

The problem is pervasive in Jordan. Norma Khouri, who recounted the death of her friend in the book *Honor Lost: Love and Death in Modern-Day Jordan*, writes, "Using just the published figures, each week one Jordanian woman is murdered for losing her chastity, whether she's a victim of rumor or a victim of rape. As with [her deceased friend] Dalia, the mere suspicion that she has lost her virginity can lead to a girl's, or woman's, murder."[**]

Queen Noor made the crisis of honor killings central to her role as a monarch, and she fought hard to change the laws that protected the murderers, but the Jordanian Parliament continued to support maintaining the law as part of the constitution.[***]

[*] Queen Noor, *Leap of Faith*, p. 388.

[**] Norma Khouri. *Honor Lost: Love and Death in Modern-day Jordan*. New York: Atria Books, 2003, p.193.

[***] Queen Noor, *Leap of Faith*, p. 388–389.

In October 1998, a desperate Clinton called Hussein's hospital suite at the Mayo Clinic to speak to the king with whom he had always enjoyed a close working and personal relationship. The two men thought alike, and both wanted a lasting peace for the region. Hussein agreed to fly to the Wye Plantation and help in the negotiations, and his doctors granted him permission. He left on October 18, and upon his arrival, was briefed on the situation. At any given moment, the Israelis threatened to leave; the Americans seemed deeply discouraged, and the Palestinians were trying to forge a treaty that would give them hope for future independence. Hussein was intensely involved in what was happening, while Noor watched over him carefully to be sure he was not overexerting himself. Hussein spoke to the negotiators present, saying, "You cannot afford to fail. . . . You owe this to your people, to your children, to future generations."[189] A couple of days later, a humble agreement was reached by which the Israelis would return a small portion of land to the Palestinians, thus keeping the peace process alive. When the signing of the Wye Memorandum took place at the White House on October 23, 1998, King Hussein was there, shrunken and frail looking, but speaking in a strong voice. It was generally agreed that the success of the peace deal was owed to the presence of the king, who had gone the distance for peace despite his fragile health. "The ailing Hussein joined the [Wye Summit] talks," says writer Alexander Bligh, author of *The Political Legacy of King Hussein,* "and indeed contributed to the signing of an agreement in order to eliminate one more source of concern for Jordan: the continued stalemate between Israel and the Palestinians."[190]

8

Flying Solo
1999–2004

When King Hussein delivered his speech at the signing of the Wye Summit Accords in October 1998, the world reeled in shock over his diminished appearance. The charismatic, olive-skinned king of Jordan, who enjoyed flying planes, riding motorcycles, and sailing in Aqaba, was a shriveled, pale version of his former self. However, a month later, he announced on Jordan television that doctors had found no further evidence of cancer in his body. It seemed he had beaten the disease. He celebrated his sixty-third birthday with family at the Mayo Clinic, which had declared him to be in complete remission.[191] After a stay of five months and a rigorous treatment of chemotherapy and bone marrow testing, Hussein and Noor left the Mayo Clinic.[192]

On January 19, 1999, Hussein finally returned home to Jordan, aboard a Jordanian Gulfstream 4 aircraft. Noor recalled:

[After leaving England,] we were immediately picked up by an RAF fighter escort from the Sixth Squadron and then, as we passed into France, by a French fighter escort. Over Italy we were joined by an Italian fighter escort, over Israeli airspace by an Israeli fighter escort, and then, for the last leg home, we were accompanied by Jordanian fighter planes. In spite of his immense fatigue, Hussein piloted for the entire trip. . . . The motorcade in the sky was the greatest possible tribute for my aviator husband.[193]

As soon as he descended from the aircraft, a fatigued Hussein knelt and prayed, accompanied by Noor and others who had escorted him home.[194] When he finally spoke to the press, Hussein made "generous personal references" to an embarrassed Noor, expressing his gratitude to the wife who had stood by him during his difficult ordeal.[195]

However, the media was once again spreading unflattering rumors about the queen. One rumor claimed that she wanted her husband to name their eldest son Hamzah as Crown Prince, rather than Hussein's brother Hassan, the current Crown Prince, or Prince Abdullah, Hussein's eldest son (by his second wife, Princess Muna). "There were reports," Noor wrote, "that I was Jewish and related somehow to Rabin, and that I, backed by American Zionists, was tirelessly campaigning to have Hamzah replace my husband's brother as Crown Prince."[196] Noor was, once again, hurt by the allegations, but stayed silent to avoid further complicating the story.

Hussein did eventually hold a private meeting with his younger brother Hassan, during which he announced his decision to name his son Abdullah as the successor to the throne. Writer Hal Marcovitz explains that the choice of replacing Hassan as Crown Prince seemed inevitable: "Over the years, Hassan had never endeared himself to the Jordanian people and often angered Hussein by meddling in the affairs of the army. Hassan was also believed to be cold toward Queen Noor," although Noor never admits to the alleged tension between herself and her brother-in-law.[197] In the end, Noor was pleased with Hussein's decision, and she gave Abdullah and and his wife Rania her full support. She was also pleased that Hamzah had not been named successor. Her husband had become king at the age of eighteen, and Noor wanted her own son to graduate from the university and live independently before delving more deeply into public service.[198]

It was not long after the decision about the succession was made that Hussein and Noor learned that his cancer had returned.[199] They opted to return to the Mayo Clinic for another bone marrow transplant, but not before the king wrote a lengthy letter to Hassan, which would be read on Jordanian television after his departure from Amman to the United States.[200] In the letter, Hussein refers specifically to Noor's strength and to the injustice she endured because of the vicious gossip reported by the Jordanian and international press:

> She brought happiness and cared for me during my illness with the utmost loving affection. She, the Jordanian, who belongs to this country with every fiber of her being, holds her head high in the defense and service of the country's interest. She is the mother who devotes all her efforts to her family. We have grown together in soul and mind, and she has had to endure a great deal of hardship to ensure that I was being attended to. And she, like me, also endured many anxieties and shocks, but always placed her faith in God and hid her tears behind smiles. She also has not escaped the arrows of criticism.

Why not? Because there are climbers who want to reach for the summit, and when the fever was getting high some people thought it was their chance.[201]

In Minnesota, Noor was informed by doctors that Hussein's condition was precipitously dangerous. Desperately trying to hold herself together, she recorded in her journal, "I am not ready to lose the light of my life."[202]

Hussein endured new rounds of chemotherapy, and seemed to do well at first, but eventually began "to talk less and less and seemed to retreat into himself."[203] His wife and children stayed by his bedside in shifts, and they all prayed desperately for his recovery. For Noor, it was an especially difficult time. She not only suffered from her own insecurities and fears, but, as she records in her memoir, she was intensely conscious of everyone else's suffering. She served as a rock upon whom all of the king's children could depend. When it became clear that Hussein, now on a respirator, was not going to recover, it was Noor who quietly decided that she would take her husband home to die.

"If we are losing this battle," she thought, "it is not going to be lost in Rochester, Minnesota. . . . He belongs at home with his Jordanian family."[204] Back in Amman, Hussein lay unconscious in a room in the King Hussein Medical Center. Noor, accompanied by Princes Feisal, Ali, Hamzah, and Hashim, spoke to the thousands of people faithfully keeping vigil in the rain. Noor asked the crowds to pray for Hussein, for his recovery and his spirit.[205]

But on February 7, 1999, the battle ended. Hussein died with his family surrounding him, his hand clasped in Noor's.

The king's funeral brought dignitaries and heads of state from around the world to Amman, allies and political enemies alike. Among those attending were American President Bill Clinton (who had brought Noor's parents to Amman with him on Air Force One) and Hosni Mubarak, the Egyptian president. "The people of Jordan were stricken with grief," writes Hal Marcovitz, author of a book on Jordan's history, "Jordanians wept in sorrow and filled mosques to pray for the soul of the dead king."[206]

In Muslim tradition, the dead are not embalmed, so they are buried as soon as possible, before sunset. Usually only men attend the burial ceremonies, but just as she had attended her own wedding, Noor was also present at the funeral of her husband. The break with tradition, not surprisingly, again provoked unfavorable media coverage. But as Noor recorded in her memoir, "Jordanians had an infinite capacity for compassion," and she was confident that they would not fault her.[207]

As painful as it was, Hussein's funeral strengthened her. "From that moment on, I knew I would never fear death," she also wrote, "but see it as a chance for reunion."[208]

KEEPING THE FAITH

Since Hussein's death, a lot has changed for Queen Noor, who now shares her royal titles with the young Queen Rania, the wife of King Abdullah. Though Noor is still very much in the public spotlight, she has more time to spend on activities that transcend the chaos that accompanies political affairs at the Jordanian royal court. In 2003, she published a memoir, *Leap of Faith: Memoirs of an Unexpected Life*, which the public received hungrily. In some ways, her life has not changed at all. Gossip and controversy continue to plague Noor. When her memoir was released in 2003, several groups and individuals attacked it because of her frank discussions of politics. She has also been criticized in the West for her recent commentaries on the political situation in the Middle East, most notably over the 2003 U.S.-led war against Iraq, which led to the toppling of Saddam Hussein's government. "As a woman and mother and a humanitarian," said Noor, "I am devastated by the impact on men, women and children in Iraq and also

On February 7, 1999, after several battles with cancer, King Hussein died in a Jordanian hospital with Queen Noor and family members constantly at his side. In a ceremony held on the first anniversary of the monarch's death, Queen Noor (right) and Queen Rania (wife of King Hussein's son and successor, King Abdullah II) offer prayers at the royal cemetery in Amman.

throughout the region." [209] This seemingly innocuous state-ment angered many in the West, who saw it as an attack on the foreign policy of the United States by the American-born queen. However, Noor had never been one to limit herself to "safe," neutral subjects. From her youth, she had engaged in issues so volatile that they threatened to rip apart society's fabric: civil rights, the Vietnam War, poverty, the Arab-Israeli conflict, and many others.

QUEEN RANIA

Just before his death, King Hussein changed the order of succession to the throne from his brother Prince Hassan to his first-born son, Prince Abdullah, suprising Jordan and the world at large. Perhaps most surprised of all was the prince, an army officer who had lived his entire life assuming that he would never have the burden of being king. Suddenly, Abdullah and his young wife Rania were thrust into the very bright glare of the public eye.

Once again, Jordan had a new queen. And, at 28 years of age, Queen Rania was a completely new kind of queen. She built on and expanded the role Noor had developed as a working queen and immediately asserted herself as an intelligent, educated spokesperson for Jordan. Rania has taken up many of Queen Noor's causes, including stopping honor killings and turning women's handicrafts into income-generating enterprises. But Queen Rania has gone even further; she has made child abuse a topic of national discussion, and is working to advance the cause of women and children in Jordan through her work in the field of microfinance (a policy that gives credit to poor women so that they can start their own businesses) and other areas.

Admittedly, Queen Rania's achievements would not be possible without Queen Noor as a forerunner. However, Rania's success as queen has much to do with her unique ability to appeal both to the West (a skill particularly significant in gaining finanical support from these countries) and the Arab world. Tall, elegant, and beautiful, Rania looks, as the society magazine *Vanity Fair* notes, "supermodel gorgeous,"* giving her an advantage with a Western culture obsessed with beauty and the glamour of royalty. But Rania is also a woman of

Today, Noor continues to live with the optimism that marked her remarkable years with Hussein. She also actively embraces causes and projects that reflect Hussein's vision for

Palestinian origin, whose native language is Arabic, unlike her husband, King Abdullah II, whose mother (King Hussein's second wife, Queen Muna) was British and whose first language is English (although his Arabic is improving). Given that Jordan is a country where the majority of people are Palestinian, Queen Rania has done wonders to downplay her husband's Western upbringing.

The queen was born Rania Al Yasin in 1970 in Kuwait, where her family lived until Iraq invaded the country in 1990 and they fled, like so many others, to Jordan during the Gulf War. Rania graduated from the American University in Cairo, Egypt, with a degree in business administration and worked for Citibank and Apple Computer before marrying Abdullah Al Hussein in 1993. The couple has three children: Prince Hussein (born in 1994), Princess Iman (born in 1996), and Princess Salma (born in 2000).

Queen Rania is an active mother to her three children, often picking them up from school and supervising their homework each night. She has been the president of the Arab Women's Summit and an active member of numerous other international and national organizations. Queen Rania serves as a wonderful role model for women in the Arab world and beyond. As Juan Somavia, the director general of the UN's International Labor Office said as he introduced her to speak in 2003, "It's quite extraordinary, the manner in which the world listens to [Queen Rania]."** As she and King Abdullah II lead Jordan into the twenty-first century, Queen Rania seems to have just what it takes to keep the world's attention.

* Leslie Bennetts "Letter from Amman." *Vanity Fair*, September 2003, p. 254.
** Ibid., p. 269.

Queen Noor continues to reinforce her commitment to peace and tolerance, with a frankness that has made her both an admired and controversial figure. She wrote a memoir of her surprising story, *Keep the Faith: Memoirs of an Unexpected Life*, and spent much of 2003 promoting the book, as photographed here at a German bookseller.

the Middle East. In 1999, King Abdullah established the King Hussein Foundation, an organization "dedicated to give meaningful expression to the late King's humanitarian vision and legacy with emphasis on democracy, peace, education, leadership, health, and the environment." Quite fittingly, Queen Noor was named the chairperson of the foundation.[210]

She sees her work on behalf of peace and justice simply as the fulfillment of the mission she shared with her husband. It is work that, despite his early death, must continue in order to make peace in the region more than a dream. "I pray that his legacy of love, tolerance, and peace lives on in all of us—it is his gift and challenge for which I will be eternally grateful and will seek to uphold in my life and work."[211] Indeed, her work continues to make a difference in the lives of many, and her intelligence, strength, humanity, and grace are inspirational.

Chronology

1951 Lisa Najeeb Halaby, the future Queen Noor, is born on August 23, 1951, in Washington, D.C. She is the first of three children for Najeeb and Doris Halaby.

1969 Enters Princeton University as part of its first co-educational class.

1971 Takes a year off from Princeton to fly to Aspen and works a variety of jobs. Also works for the Aspen Institute, a nonprofit organization, and makes important connections.

1974 Graduates from Princeton and begins working for the firm Llewelyn-Davis, which sends her to work on a project in Australia.

1975 Moves to Tehran for a year while working for the Aspen Institute.

1976 Makes her first trip to Jordan. Months later, Lisa returns with her father and meets King Hussein for the first time.

1978 Has a brief, three-week courtship with King Hussein before marrying him and becoming Noor Al Hussein, queen of Jordan.

1979 Suffers a miscarriage. Establishes the Royal Endowment for Culture and Education.

1980 First-born child, Prince Hamzah, is born on March 29. Launches the Arab Children's Congress. Makes first visit to the United States since becoming queen.

1981 Gives first political speech at Georgetown University in Washington, D.C. Her second son, Hashim, is born on June 10. Launches annual arts and crafts fair, the Jerash Festival.

1983 Iman, Noor's first daughter, is born on April 24.

1986 Noor's fourth and last child, Raiyah, is born on February 9.

1990 Iraq invades Kuwait, causing millions of Kuwaiti refugees to pour into Jordan. Noor supervises the refugee camps.

1991   The Gulf War ends. Rumors circulate about an affair between King Hussein and a government employee, causing strain to Noor and Hussein's marriage.

1992   Noor accompanies Hussein to the Mayo Clinic in the United States after doctors discover an abnormal growth in his kidneys containg precancerous cells. An operation removes one of his kidneys as well as the precancerous cells.

1998   Doctors at the Mayo Clinic inform Hussein and Noor that Hussein has non-Hodgkins lymphoma. Noor stays at Hussein's side during the months he undergoes chemotherapy in Minnesota.

1999   Noor's husband, King Hussein, dies on February 7. Breaking with Muslim tradition, Noor attends the funeral.

2003   Noor publishes her memoir, *Leap of Faith: Memoirs of an Unexpected Life.*

Notes

CHAPTER 1

1. Her Majesty Queen Noor Al Hussein, *Leap of Faith.* New York: Miramax, 2003, p.105.
2. Ibid., p. 105–106.
3. Ibid., p.114.
4. Ibid., p.125.
5. Castalia Systems, "History of Aleppo." Syria Gate, *http://www.syriagate.com/Syria/ about/cities/Aleppo/history.htm.*
6. Lynn Simarski, "The Lure of Aleppo." Aramco World, *http://almashriq.hiof.no/syria/900/ the_lure_of_aleppo.*
7. Queen Noor, *Leap of Faith,* p. 10.
8. Ibid.
9. Ibid.
10. Ibid., p. 11.
11. Ibid., p. 12.
12. Ibid.
13. Sam Blair, "Legends: Najeeb Halaby and Plane Truth." *Private Clubs,* November/December 2000. *http://www.privateclubs.com/archi ves/2000-nov-dec/life_legends.htm*
14. Queen Noor, *Leap of Faith,* p. 12.
15. Ibid., p.13.
16. Albert Hourani, *A History of the Arab Peoples.* New York: Warner Books, 1992, p. 356.
17. Queen Noor, *Leap of Faith,* p.13–14.
18. Ibid., p.15.
19. Ibid.
20. Ibid., p.14.
21. Ibid., p.15.

CHAPTER 2

22. Queen Noor, *Leap of Faith,* p.16.
23. Ibid., p.17.
24. Ibid., p.15.
25. Ibid., p.18.
26. Ibid. p.19.
27. Ibid.
28. Ibid., p.18.
29. Ibid., p.23.
30. Ibid.
31. Ibid., p.24.
32. James Meredith, "Letter to the U.S. Department of Justice." John F. Kennedy Library, *http://www.jfklibrary.org/ meredith/jm_02.html.*
33. Jessica McElrath, "James Meredith's Admission to Ole Mississippi." About.com: African-American History. *http://afroamhistory. about.com/cs/jamesmeredith/a/ jamesmeredith.htm.*
34. Queen Noor, *Leap of Faith,* p. 21.
34. Ibid.
35. Ibid., p. 25.
36. Ibid.
37. Ibid., p. 26.
38. Ibid. p. 27.
39. Ibid.
40. Ibid., p. 28.
41. Ibid., p. 29.
42. Ibid.
43. Ibid., p. 30.
44. Ibid., p. 31.
45. Ibid.

CHAPTER 3

46. Queen Noor, *Leap of Faith,* p. 30.
47. Ibid., p. 32.
48. Ibid.
49. Ibid.
50. Ibid.
51. Ibid., p. 33.
52. Ibid., p. 36.
53. Ibid., p. 38.
54. Ibid., p. 44.
55. Ibid., p. 5.
56. Ibid., p. 7.
57. Ibid., p. 46.
58. Ibid.
59. Ibid.
60. Ibid.
61. The Gale Group, "Queen Noor al Hussein," Farmington Hills, Minn.: Biography Resource Center, 2003, p. 2.
62. Queen Noor, *Leap of Faith,* p. 48.
63. Ibid., p. 50

64. Ibid., p. 68.
65. Ibid., p.79

CHAPTER 4

66. Hal Marcovitz, *Jordan.* Creation of the Modern Middle East Series. Philadelphia: Chelsea House, 2003, p. 45.
67. Ibid., p. 46.
68. Ibid., p. 59.
69. "Biographical Information: King Abdullah Al-Hussein (1882–1951)." A Living Tribute to the Legacy of King Hussein I. *http://www.kinghussein.gov.jo/kingabdullah.html.*
70. "The Hashemite Kingdom of Jordan." A Living Tribute to the Legacy of King Hussein I. *http://www.kinghussein.gov.jo/his_kings.html*
71. Robert B. Satloff, *From Abdullah to Hussein: Jordan in Transition.* New York: Oxford University Press, 1994, p. 20–21.
72. Ibid., p. 21.
73. Ralph H. Magnus, "Jordan." *Encyclopedia Americana.* Grolier Online, 2002. *http://www.ea.grolier.com* (May 2, 2003).
74. Satloff, *From Abdullah to Hussein: Jordan in Transition,* p.107.
75. Alexander Bligh, *The Political Legacy of King Hussein,* Portland, Oregon: Sussex Academic Press, 2002, p. 8.
76. Arthur Goldschmidt Jr., *A Concise History of the Middle East,* 7th ed. Boulder, Colo.: Westview Press, 2002, p. 287.
77. Magnus, "Jordan," *Encyclopedia Americana.*
78. Ibid.
79. Coleman South, *Jordan.* New York: Marshall Cavendish, 1997, 42.
80. Goldschmidt, *A Concise History of the Middle East,* p. 229–230.
81. Ibid., p. 317.

82. Ibid., p. 350.
83. Queen Noor, *Leap of Faith,* p. 81.
84. Ibid., p. 90.
85. Ibid., p. 81.
86. Ibid., p. 91.
87. Ibid., p. 94
88. Ibid., p. 97.
89. Ibid., p. 96.
90. Ibid., p. 95.
91. Dorothy Rompalske, "The All-American Girl Who Became Queen." *Biography Magazine.* 1, no. 9 (September 1997).
92. Queen Noor, *Leap of Faith,* p. 97.
93. Ibid., p. 100.
94. Ibid., p. 101.
95. The Gale Group, "Queen Noor al Hussein," p. 2.
96. Queen Noor, *Leap of Faith,* p. 102.
97. Ibid., p. 130.

CHAPTER 5

98. Queen Noor, *Leap of Faith,* p. 103.
99. Ibid., p. 98.
100. Ibid., p. 100.
101. Kim Hubbard, Simon Perry, et al. "Painful Passage." *People*, March 1, 1999, p.1.
102. Ibid.
103. The Gale Group, "Queen Noor al Hussein," p. 2.
104. Rompalske, "The All-American Girl Who Became Queen," p. 1.
105. Goldschmidt, *A Concise History of the Middle East,* p. 372.
106. Queen Noor, *Leap of Faith,* p.155–158.
107. Ibid., p. 160–161.
108. Ibid., p. 161.
109. Ibid., p. 183.
110. "Personal Profile: Her Majesty Queen Noor of Jordan." Official Website of Her Majesty Queen Noor. *http://www.noor.gov.jo/personal_profile.htm.*
111. Queen Noor, *Leap of Faith,* p. 176.
112. Ibid.

Notes

113. Ibid., p. 177.
114. "Personal Profile: Her Majesty Queen Noor of Jordan." Official Website of Her Majesty Queen Noor. *http://www.noor.gov.jo/ personal_profile.htm.*
115. Ibid.
116. Queen Noor, *Leap of Faith*, p. 189.
117. Hal Marcovitz, *Jordan*, p. 102.
118. Queen Noor, *Leap of Faith*, p.193.
119. Ibid., p. 194.
120. Ibid., p. 204 and Hal Marcovitz, *Jordan*, p. 95.
121. Ibid., p. 211–212.
122. Ibid., p. 211.
123. Ibid., p. 200, 217.
124. Ibid., p. 217.
125. "Lebanese Civil War." *Encyclopedia of the Orient. http://i-cias.com/e.o/index.htm.* June 2, 2003.
126. Queen Noor, *Leap of Faith*, p. 217.
127. Ibid., p. 219.
128. Ibid., p. 221.
129. Ibid., p. 137.
130. Ibid.
131. Ibid.

CHAPTER 6

132. Ibid., p. 265.
133. Ibid., p. 263–264.
134. Ibid., p. 264.
135. Ibid., p. 265–266.
136. Ibid., p. 246.
137. Ibid., p. 272
138. Ibid.
139. Ibid.
140. "Jerash Festival." Website of the Jordanian Ministry of Tourism and Antiquities. *http://www.tourism. jo/tourism/HistoricalSites/ jerashFestival.asp.* June 2, 2003.
141. Queen Noor, *Leap of Faith*, p. 271.
142. Ibid., p. 289.
143. Ibid., p. 291.
144. Ibid., p. 292
145. Ibid., p. 291.

146. Ibid., p. 294.
147. Ibid., p. 294–295.
148. Ibid., p. 303–304.
149. Ibid., p. 305.
150. Ibid., p. 306.
151. Ibid., p. 303.
152. "Flashback: Invasion of Kuwait." BBC News Online. August 1, 2000. *http://news.bbc.co.uk/2/hi/ middle_east/856009.stm.*
153. Queen Noor, *Leap of Faith*, p. 306.
154. Ibid., p. 309.
155. Ibid., p. 311.
156. Ibid.
157. Ibid., p. 312.
158. Ibid., p. 310.
159. Ibid.
160. Ibid.
161. Ibid., p. 314.
162. Ibid. p. 316.
163. Ibid., p. 317.
164. Ibid. p. 318.
165. "Flashback: Invasion of Kuwait." BBC News Online. August 1, 2000. *http://news.bbc.co.uk/2/hi/ middle_east/856009stm.*
166. Queen Noor, *Leap of Faith*, p. 331.
167. Ibid., p. 333.

CHAPTER 7

168. Queen Noor, *Leap of Faith*, p. 341
169. Ibid., p. 347–348.
170. Ibid., p. 348.
171. Ibid.
172. Ibid., p. 351–352.
173. Ibid. p. 353.
174. Ibid.
175. Ibid., p. 354.
176. Ibid., p. 357–358.
177. Ibid., p. 361.
178. Ibid., p. 387.
179. Ibid., p. 251.
180. Ibid., p. 400.
181. Ibid., p. 401.
183. Ibid., p. 403.
184. Ibid., p. 404
185. Ibid.

186. Ibid., p. 407.
187. Ibid., p. 412
188. Her Majesty Queen Noor Al-Hussein. Address to the 1st Middle East Conference on Landmines Injury & Rehabilitation. Amman, 11 July 1998. *http://www.go.com.jo/QNoorjo/main/apmspch.htm.*
189. Queen Noor, *Leap of Faith*, p. 415.
190. Alexander Bligh, *The Political Legacy of King Hussein*, p. 199–200.

CHAPTER EIGHT

191. Queen Noor, *Leap of Faith*, p. 417–418.
192. Ibid., p. 419.
193. Ibid., p. 423.
194. Ibid., p. 424.
195. Ibid.
196. Ibid., p. 418.
197. Marcovitz, *Jordan*, p.112.
198. Queen Noor, *Leap of Faith*, p. 426.
199. Ibid., p. 427.
200. Ibid.
201. Ibid., p. 428–429.
202. Ibid., p. 429.
203. Ibid., p. 430.
204. Ibid., p. 431.
205. Ibid., p. 432.
206. Marcovitz, *Jordan*, p. 113.
207. Queen Noor, *Leap of Faith*, p. 434.
208. Ibid., p. 435.
209. "Queen Noor: Pushing for Peace." BBC News Online. *http://news.bbc.co.uk/2/hi/programmes/breakfast/2927501.stm.*
210. "Personal Profile: Her Majesty Queen Noor of Jordan." Official Website of Her Majesty Queen Noor. *http://www.noor.gov.jo/personal_profile.htm.*
211. Queen Noor, *Leap of Faith*, p. 440.

Bibliography

Bligh, Alexander. *The Political Legacy of King Hussein*. Portland, Ore.: Sussex Academic Press, 2002.

Goldschmidt, Arthur, Jr. *A Concise History of the Middle East*, 7th ed. Boulder, Colo.: Westview Press, 2002.

Hubbard, Kim, Simon Perry, et al. "Painful Passage." *People*, March 1, 1999 (Academic Search Premier Database).

Al Hussein, Her Majesty Queen Noor. *Leap of Faith: Memoirs of an Unexpected Life*. New York: Miramax Books, 2003.

Khouri, Norma. *Honor Lost: Love and Death in Modern-day Jordan*. New York: Atria Books, 2003.

Marcovitz, Hal. *Jordan*. Creation of the Modern Middle East Series. Philadelphia: Chelsea House, 2003.

Rompalske, Dorothy. "The All-American Girl Who Became Queen." *Biography Magazine*. 1, no. 9 (September 1997).

Satloff, Robert B. *From Abdullah to Hussein: Jordan in Transition*. New York: Oxford University Press, 1994.

South, Coleman. *Jordan*. Cultures of the World Series. New York: Marshall Cavendish, 1997.

Suleiman, Michael. *The Arabs in the Mind of America*. Brattleboro, Vt.: Amana Books, 1988.

Websites

Blair, Sam. "Legends: Najeeb Halaby and Plane Truth." *Private Clubs*, November/December 2000. *http://www.privateclubs.com/archives/2000-nov-dec/life_legends.htm*.

"Flashback: Invasion of Kuwait." BBC Online. 1 August 2000. *http://news.bbc.co.uk/2/hi/middle_east/856009stm*.

"Honor Killings." *New York Times*. 12 November 2000. Found in ProQuest Direct Database. *http://www.pqdweb.com*.

Al Hussein, Her Majesty Queen Noor. Address to the 1st Middle East Conference on Landmines Injury & Rehabilitation. Amman, 11 July 1998. *http://www.go.com. jo/QNoorjo/main/apmspch.htm*.

"Jerash Festival." Website of the Jordanian Ministry of Tourism and Antiquities. *http://www.tourism.jo/tourism/HistoricalSites/jerashFestival.asp*. 2 June 2003.

"Lebanese Civil War." *Encyclopedia of the Orient. http://i-cias.com/e.o/ index.htm.* 2 June 2003.

Magnus, Ralph H. "Jordan." *Encyclopedia Americana.* Grolier Online, 2002. *http://www.ea.grolier.com* (2 May 2003).

"Personal Profile: Her Majesty Queen Noor of Jordan." Official Website of Her Majesty Queen Noor. *http://www.noor.gov.jo/personal_profile.htm.*

"Projects: Her Majesty Queen Noor of Jordan." Official Website of Her Majesty Queen Noor. *http://www.noor.gov.jo/projects.htm.*

"Queen Noor al Hussein." *Biography Resource Center Online.* Gale Group, 2003. Reproduced in *Biography Resource Center.* Farmington Hills, Mich.: The Gale Group, 2003. *http://www.galenet.com/ servlet/BioRC.*

"Timeline: Iraq." BBC Online. May 23, 2003. *http://news.bbc.co.uk/2/hi/ middle_east/737483.stm.* 3 June 2003.

Further Reading

Amin, Mohamed, Duncan Willets, and Sam Kiley. *Journey Through Jordan*. Northampton, Mass.: Interlink Publishing Group, 2000.

El-Azhary Sonbol, Amira. *Women of the Jordan: Islam, Labor, and the Law. Gender, Culture, and Politics of the Middle East Series*. Syracuse, N.Y.: Syracuse University Press, 2003.

Borgia, E. *Jordan Past and Present: Petra, Jerash, Amman*. New York: Oxford University Press, 2003.

Bennetts, Leslie. "Letter from Amman." *Vanity Fair*, September 2003. pp. 254–272.

Dallas, Roland. *King Hussein: A Life on the Edge*. New York: Fromm Intl, 1999.

Al Hussein, Her Majesty Queen Noor. *Leap of Faith: Memoirs of an Unexpected Life*. New York: Miramax Books, 2003.

Joffe, George. *Jordan In Transition*. New York: Palgrave Macmillan, 2002.

Al Madfai, Madhia Rashid. *Jordan, the United States and the Middle East Peace Process, 1974–1991*. New York: Cambridge University Press, 1993.

Rogan, Eugene. *Frontiers of the State in the Late Ottoman Empire: Transjordan, 1850–1921*. New York: Cambridge University Press, 2000.

Salibi, Kamal. *A Modern History of Jordan*. New York: I. B. Tauris & Co Ltd, 1993.

Index

on becoming King, 42
his children, 48–50, 58
his courtship with Lisa,
35–37
his death, 93
devotion to his country, 4
his failing health, 81, 85–86
the honeymoon, 2–4
and letter to Hassan, 92–93
his marriage to Lisa, 51–53
the Mayo Clinic, 90–91
the Palestine-Israeli conflict,
43–46
and Rabin's funeral, 84
on Saddam Hussein, 72 73
his training to assume
throne, 42
and war in Iraq, 75
his wives, 4, 48
Hussein, Faisal, 39–40
Hussein, Hashim, 63–64
Hussein, Haya, 4
Hussein, Iman, 64
Hussein, Raiyah Al, 68
Hussein, Saddam, 72
and defeat of Iraqi Army,
75
on speaking out against
America, 72–73
Hussein, Sharif, 39–40

Institute of Defense Analyses,
27
International Organization
for Migration, 76
Iraq, 73–74
Israeli Knesset, 46

Jerash Festival, 70–71
Johnson, Lyndon, 22

Jordan
architecture of, 32–33
freed Turkish control, 39
and refugees, 75–76

Kennedy, John F. , 16
and appointment of Najeeb,
17
assassination of, 20–21
his optimism for America's
youth, 19–20
Kent State University, 27
Khouri, Norma, 88
King Hussein Foundation, 98
King Hussein Medical Center,
93
King, Martin Luther Jr., 21–22
the 1963 March on
Washington, 23
Koen, Urban, 9
Kuwait
invasion of, 73–74

Landmines, 86–87
Landmine Survivors Network,
87
Lautenberg, Frank, 77
Lawrence of Arabia, 40
Leap of Faith, (Queen Noor),
94, 98
Lebanese Civil War, 64–65
Lebanon, 5–6
Lincoln, Abraham, 22
Lindberg, Charles, 9
Llewelyn-Davis Firm, 28
Lockheed Corporation, 9

Marcovitz, Hal, 92
on King Hussein's death,
94

Index

Index

Credits

page:

3: Courtesy of the Office of Her Majesty Queen Noor

13: Courtesy of the Office of Her Majesty Queen Noor

17: Courtesy of the Office of Her Majesty Queen Noor

29: Courtesy of the Office of Her Majesty Queen Noor

36: Courtesy of the Office of Her Majesty Queen Noor

39: Associated Press Graphics

52: Courtesy of the Office of Her Majesty Queen Noor

58: Courtesy of the Office of Her Majesty Queen Noor

71: Courtesy of the Office of Her Majesty Queen Noor

84: © LANGEVIN JACQUES/CORBIS SYGMA

95: Associated Press, AP/Yousef Allan

98: Associated Press, AP/Franka Bruns

Cover: Courtesy of the Office of Her Majesty Queen Noor

About the Author

Susan Muaddi Darraj (*http://www.SusanMuaddiDarraj.com*) is freelance writer based in Baltimore, Maryland. She has authored numerous articles, short fiction, and books, and she also teaches college-level English and writing courses. She is also the author of *John F. Kennedy* in Chelsea House's GREAT AMERICAN PRESIDENTS series.